Trade, Territory and Technology

Economic Crisis in the Global Economy

Trade, Territory and Technology

Economic Crisis in the Global Economy

Shrinivas Tripathi

New Century Publications
New Delhi, India

NEW CENTURY PUBLICATIONS
4800/24, Bharat Ram Road,
Ansari Road, Daryaganj,
New Delhi – 110 002 (India)

Tel.: 011-2324 7798, 4358 7398, 6539 6605
Fax: 011-4101 7798
E-mail: indiatax@vsnl.com • info@newcenturypublications.com
www.newcenturypublications.com

Editorial office:
LG–7, Aakarshan Bhawan,
4754-57/23, Ansari Road, Daryaganj,
New Delhi – 110 002

Tel.: 011-4356 0919

First Published: **2012**

ISBN: **978-81-7708-299-9**

Published by New Century Publications and printed at Salasar Imaging Systems, New Delhi.

Designs: Patch Creative Unit, New Delhi.

PRINTED IN INDIA

Dedicated to my father

Late Sri Satya Narayan Tripathi

Declarations

It is declared to the best of the knowledge and belief of the author that:

1. It is entirely the responsibility of the author for author's views and comments in the book and Governments are in no way concerned with the publication of the book.
2. The book does not contain any statement of fact or opinion which has any adverse criticism of any current or recent policy or action of the State Government or Central Government or Government of any other State or local authority.
3. The book is written with the aid of knowledge acquired by the author in the course of his service, but it reveals the author's scholarly study of the subjects and the work neither has nor is likely to have any connection with the author's official position.
4. The book is related to the general welfare of the humanity as a whole, assuming all the people, residing on the 'mother earth,' as the members of a single household.

Shrinivas Tripathi
August 15, 2009
Lucknow

About the Book

This book is an attempt to look at the structural and functional changes occurring in the global economic system in the wake of liberalization, privatization and globalization wave sweeping across the world economies.

People in developing countries have lost confidence in the existing international institutions—which are supposed to be the protectors—because at the time of the crisis they seem helpless in protecting the interests of poor economies. The institutions like International Monetary Fund (IMF) and the World Bank did not do enough during Asian Crisis of the last century. They were again not forthcoming when the Economic Crisis (2008) hit the world economies. Problems like poverty and unemployment in underdeveloped countries cannot be solved by one nation but need concerted efforts of the world as a whole. Therefore, there is a need for Global Democratic Government to make the world happier and a prosperous home of human beings.

About the Author

Shrinivas Tripathi is presently posted as Finance and Accounts Officer, Irrigation Department, Lucknow, Uttar Pradesh.

He did his Post-graduation in Geography and LL.B. from Allahabad University. He was selected for Uttar Pradesh Provincial Civil Services Examination in 1998 and was allotted Finance and Accounts Service cadre. After training, he was posted as Treasury Officer at Treasury Office, Jawahar Bhawan, Lucknow.

He attended Indian History Congress held at Shanti Niketan, West Bengal, in 2006 and Oriental Conference at Jammu University, Jammu in the same year.

Foreword

After fall of Grenada of the Arabs at the hands of Spain, it became the most powerful monarchy of Europe in 15th century, though it was not parallel to India and China at that time. Prosperity of the East allured the West and compelled them to come through any route, the land or sea as the air route was absent at that time. The land route was closed by Ottoman Turks, so the sea route was chosen as an alternative after 1453. Columbus, with the help of some private investors of Europe especially Italians, crossing the Atlantic Ocean reached in America in 1492, then unknown to the Europeans. Thereafter, the Europeans started colonization in Americas on the cost of the native dwellers and with the help of the African slaves. After the fall of Constantinople to the hands of Ottoman Turks which was the end of the medieval period and beginning of the modern age in the World history, the European colonizers wiped out the deep rooted cultures of Peru and Mexico in American continent.

Portuguese Vasco-da-Gama reached at Calicut on Malabar Coast in 1498 and at Goa in 1510 of India, via Cape of Good-Hope, the southern tip of Africa. Almost at the same time, Babar attacked on India in 1526, through land route via Khaibar and Bolan Passes of north-west India. Sher Shah Suri defeated Babar's son Humayun at the Battles of Chausa and Kannauj and compelled him to flee to Iran who returned again in 1555 and established the Mughal Dynasty in India with the capital at Delhi.

It is to be remembered that in 1570 the carrying capacity of Dutch merchant shipping was almost equal to the combined fleet of England, France and Germany. In 1565 Spain occupied Philippines and sent soldiers and Christian Missionaries to the East but the invincible 'Armada' sent by Spain to conquer England was wrecked in 1588.

Queen Elizabeth gave a Charter to the British East India Company to trade with the East in 1600 whereas the Dutch

East India Company was formed in 1602. The investors of East India Company used to get dividend up to 100 percent, 150 percent and even 200 percent annually. The profits earned from India and other parts of the British Empire were used in the development of the U.S. Railways etc.

The British, after fraudulently and camouflagingly defeating Mir Zafar, the Nawab of Bengal, in the Battle of Plessey in 1757, initiated political interference amongst the native Indian States. The trading company became governing body, after conquering and bringing India under the British-company rule the regular squeeze of the Indian resources, wealth as well as man power began in the interest of the British industries.

By the mid-19th century, the U.S. surpassed Tsarist Russia, Revolutionary Prussia and almost matched France and India in purchasing power. At that time the Indian Economy was just next to that of Britain and almost matched with that of France. By 1880s, the U.S. had undertaken the U.K., the most powerful economy of the World.

Thereafter, the World faced industrial revolutions, different depressions and booms, oil crisis and economic crises. Textile, transportation, coal and iron industries flourished with their various phases at the beginning of the British Empire in India. The geo-politics, de-colonization, neo-imperialism, multi-national corporations, inter-national economic institutions with the U.S. hegemony and public economy were the developments in the World, after Second World War.

By mid of the twentieth century, the colonies which had become unbearable and non-profitable burden of the colonizers, freedom was thrust upon them. By 1940s, the American economy had become so strong that it needed larger markets of Asia and Africa that were under the European colonial powers.

The period from 16th to 20th century was of the Americans and the Europeans with especial emphasis on cruel large scale slave trade in early years and squeezing of civilized people and nations for acquiring their wealth and land for the Europeans, whereas the present century is for conservation of the human dignity, equal distribution of wealth and opportunities as per one's need and requirement.

Today, for one group of the countries of the World, agriculture is a commercial activity with high productivity, due to their big machines and plants, whereas for the other group, it is a way of life of the people with involvement of the family members for their subsistence characterized by low production and low productivity. Almost two billion people are starving today. The West tried to solve the problem of poor nations but as a by-product of the process of the maximization of profit in the name of so-called development.

In the centre of the food problem is, ''what is lacking is not the food material, but the political will and the social commitment to fairly distribute food, regardless of the recipient's ability to pay.''

Upnishad lays down, "No one should sleep without enough food because of economic constraints or social inequality."

The water reservoirs, constructed by Rudradaman in South India and Rajput Kings at so many places of Bundelkhand of U.P. are still serving the purposes. Nawab Asaf-ud-daula of Lucknow is still remembered for providing employment to the unskilled labourer class during the famine. To test the existence of famine, construction of canals was done under the Famine Act during the British period in India, which even today is serving the purpose.

During 1965-drought conditions; particularly in Vindhyan ranges of Mirzapur district in U.P., the efforts made to provide relief were recorded by Pt. Braj Bhushan Misra '*Gramwasi*', the freedom fighter, in his daily diary, now published as '*Mere Jivan Ki Kahani*'(the story of my life).

The U.P. Drought Relief Committee was an association of the voluntary organizations under the chairmanship of Shri

A.G. Kher, former Chairman of U.P. Legislative Assembly. I had an occasion to serve as the secretary of the committee under his guidance, in the drought-hit areas. In the context of political and social commitment, I shall like to mention that during the Morarji Desai's Government a conference of the voluntary organizations of the country was called for at Vijnan Bhavan, Delhi, where I represented U.P. Drought Relief Committee.

Moreover, in the context of the food shortage the rising prices of petrol, changes in the cropping pattern in favour of corn for bio-diesel and reduction in area under rice and wheat created shortage of food grains and animal based food products and increased their prices. It became very painful not for the U.S. and other developed countries but to the other parts of the World and their people. Thus, the food in-security of the people of the World is finally due to the politico-economic reasons. The under-nourishment is prevalent in the large number of the African nations and their people.

At this point of time, 21st century World is divided into two groups; one headed by the U.S. is fully industrialized but highly dependent on the outer World for the markets. The other group has the two big economies with high population and large national markets. The conspicuous feature of the 21st century is Asia-centric development of the World with special emphasis on the welfare of the people. But decades of policy making by World Bank and the IMF have indirectly pushed the poor nations towards the self-destruction.

In early year of the third millennium, almost 40 percent of the World population is making stride in regard to the development and industrialization under the banner of BRIC, an association of Brazil, Russia, India and China. It comprises more than one-thirds of work-force, skilled and unskilled both, in the World. India and China are producing half a million scientists and engineers whereas the U.S. is producing just 60,000 in a year.

Fed up with the same old wine in the changed bottle

provided by the dominating World power, the BRIC having 40 percent of the World population and 20 percent of the World GDP, in term of purchasing power parity, in summit meet on 16th of June 2009 in Yekaterinburg, inter-alia almost directly attacked on the Western domination over International institutions, where the emerging and developing countries must have greater say and representation in the appointment of the heads of these institutions which should be open, transparent and merit based along with the comprehensive reforms in the U.N. with due status to India and Brazil where all decisions should be taken in fairer basis. But the ground reality is that the U.S. hegemony is maintained through the U.N. and the Bretton Woods institutions, though both types of institutions have lost their credibility.

Some efforts were made in the past for a Federal World Government but the progress remained nominal, moving a few steps ahead only. The previous attempts were for the formation of a union of different nations making a Federal Government. It was based on one nation one vote.

In 21st century when conservation of human dignity is got prominence, one person one vote should be the basis of the election of the World Government. The learned author, in this background, has rightly proposed directly elected Global Democratic Government based on one person one vote.

The purchasing power of the masses can be improved by giving them employment, which could not be achieved without representation of the poor people in the Global Decision-making Bodies. It will be the solution of the global problems. A democratically directly elected Global Government of one representative at every ten million population seems to be the only way to come out of the clutches of the new types of the extortions by those who have been sucking other natives' blood under different metamorphosis during the last five hundred years.

To some, the idea of such a global arrangement may seem preposterous but the fact remains that in India during the struggle for freedom, earlier in the first half of the 20th century, what to say about the outside World even in our own country people were reluctant to accept that British will leave India. But the majority of the European colonies evaporated after India's Independence and changed the political map of Asia.

Giving the details of usurpation of trade and territories and the use of their man power as slaves, author has stepwise given the details of the inhumane and crushed methods, through which the Europeans squeezed the wealth of the rest continents and made their people pauper. But after emancipating themselves from their clutches and having made their economy again stronger, almost equal to them, they will sooner than the later be ahead of them and will be in a position to solve the World problems through their global vision and representation.

Instead of clamouring inch by inch others' territories, an entire change in international order, as advocated by the writer, will not only provide economic prosperity, which is due to them for their contribution in the creation of World's wealth through their positive approach, but will also extend a helping hand for the peace of the World.

Now it is for the have-nots of the World to come forward for their economical, political, social and religious emancipation, without missing the opportunity and repeating their historical follies, that they committed during the last five hundred years and to give a new order in international affairs.

I am grateful to Pt. Shrinivas Tripathi for acceding to my request, instead of wasting his precious leisure time in unending gossips, to contribute creatively his knowledge and efforts for human welfare.

Sri Shrinivas Tripathi has done memorable service for the cause of re-emergence of the culturally high, economically strong and socially harmonious nations and proposing a world forum for the peace and really equitable distribution of wealth among all the big and the small nations.

I shall be happy if a Hindi Version of this publication could be provided for wider awareness among the masses about the facts mentioned in this work. Lastly, my Ashirwad (blessings) goes to Shrinivas for going ahead in search of peace.

Jitendra Kumar Tripathi
Life-member
Wider Association for Vedic Studies
(Formerly World Association for Vedic Studies)
Head-office- 510, Beau lieu Drive, Lafayette,
Louisiana, USA- 70508

Contents

Preface

This book is an attempt to look at the structural and functional changes occurring in the modern economic system that evolved on the debris of the medieval land based economic pattern in the 15th century. The conspicuous economic features of the modern world are prominence of the secondary and tertiary economic activities and relegation of the primary one to the back seat. The economic crisis of 2008, a great divide in the world history, is all set to bring the perceptible changes in the global economic system.

The Western capitalist economy sprouted with the discovery of the 'new lands' which opened space for trade and flourished with the emergence of the colonialism and the industrialism. It faced the 'long depression' in the last decades of the 19th century and the 'great depression' in the early 20th century. The recovery from the 'long depression' was through the expansion of the colonial markets and exploitation of the colonies. England was the first one to recover from the 'great depression' through the hidden resources of the Colonial Empire, before the depression was buried beneath the World War Second. Later on, the colonialism and the imperialism were replaced by the neo-imperialism which continued in some form up to the eruption of the economic crisis of 2008.

When economic crisis started peeping in 2007, it was supposed that the Asian economies were de-linked from the Western one and the crisis would remain confined to the West only. But it did not happen as the Western economies are not self-dependent, rather they are dependent on that of the East. The different economies in the World are intricately interwoven, interrelated and interdependent. It was supposed that in the early years of the third millennium, the global economy was driven by the conspicuous consumption of the West in general and the U.S. in particular.

There have been trade relations between the East and the West through the MNCs, Governments and other agencies.

Therefore, the sources of the earnings of the Western countries were not confined to the West only but they were outside the West in the East also. The crisis has weakened the trade and decreased the purchasing power more in the East than the West. The negligence of the poor, reflected in the reduced purchasing power, has adversely affected the rich of the World. The products of the multinational corporations and that of the rich are sold more in the poor nations where the purchasing power has evaporated from the scene. It has taken place in the West also but to a lesser degree.

During the last almost 500 years, the supply side of economics was properly taken care of whereas the demand side remained neglected. The supply in the economy was provided by the select few whereas demand was to be created by the masses which did not take place properly in the past. The wide gap between the supply and the demand of the past continued to rise till today.

Enhancement in the purchasing power increases the demand in an economy and it was never given priority and significance. It was presumed that the buying capacity of the people would increase as a by-product of the development. The MNCs and the others relied on the small groups which had purchasing power in the developing world but the price-rise in early years of the first decade of the 21st century has got reduced the group significantly. Therefore, sustainability of the business of MNCs is now threatened.

The most serious problem today is the unemployment. The MNCs have increased the production and the productivity in the economy but they could not generate employment up to the required level. The job-producing elasticity is more in the intermediate and the smaller entrepreneurs who have lost their significance in the era of the monopoly of the MNCs. The World is feeling necessity of the medium and the small entrepreneurs. The crisis has brought an issue at the surface that in the present world no event is local, everything has global ramifications. But the irony is that the champions of globalization are retracting from their global responsibilities as they have become critic of that and the follower of the protectionism.

Presently, the people have lost their confidence in the existing international institutions, which are supposed to be the protectors, because at the time of the crisis they seem helpless in protecting the interests of the people. The institutions like IMF and the World Bank have not done fairly during the Asian Crisis of the last century. The problems like unemployment and reduced purchasing power cannot be solved by one nation but they need concerted efforts of the world as a whole. Therefore, there is a need of Global Democratic Government, elected on the basis of one person one vote, as soon as possible, to make the world happier and prosperous home of the human beings.

Acknowledgements

The book is dedicated to my father late Sri Satya Narayan Tripathi, who was a teacher by profession. He fostered global outlook and vision in my personality and without his teachings and blessings the work would not have been conceived. The God bless him immortality. The compassion, tolerance and affection to the humanity reflected in my personality and the book are the boons of my mother, Shrimati Mangali Tripathi, whose blessings are still with me and I pray to the God for her long life.

The book would not have been a reality without vital and continuous support of Sri Jitendra Kumar Tripathi, life-member of Wider Association for Vedic Studies. He has always been available to me for any assistance from reading of the manuscript to the direction and guidance, at any time. He is my friend, philosopher and guide.

Lastly, the family members provided visionary, informative and literary guidance and boosted morale in every situation. My wife Pushpa Tripathi has always stood by me and shared the thoughts. My daughters Shubha, Sudha and

Tridha have been with me in every situation and my son Kaustubhmani Tripathi contributed to the work in various ways.

Lucknow **Shrinivas Tripathi**

1

Introduction

The economic crisis 2008 is deeper and wider than any crisis the World has seen before. Melancholy of the crisis was echoed in the Conference of the World Economic Forum 2009 held on the 1st February of that year in Davos, a city of Switzerland. The conference was a gathering of the business and political leaders of the World who entered in the sessions of the forum gloomy and depressed, after exchanging their views on repercussions of the crisis which had started peeping in mid-2007 in the U.S. and within a very short time had engulfed whole of the global economy, came out paralyzed with fear and pessimism.

The modern techno-scientific-capitalistic economic system which plunged into the deep crisis in 2008 was evolved through the junction and conjunction of the trade, territory and technology in the Western Europe during the 15th century after the fall of the Greco-Roman Empire. The economic institutions, which originated in the course of the Economic Revolution, gathered momentum after the Industrial Revolution in England that began with the invention of the steam power by James Watt in 1765. The use of the steam power as a driving force of the machine was the greatest technological development of the day that ushered in the mechanical power in the economic activity very first time in the history of the human development.

The cotton industry of England was the first to be benefited by the steam power. After that, the coal mining and the iron and steel industry developed in England. By mid-19th century, Europe and North and South Americas passed through the railway boom. Although technology alone did not lead to the industrialization, yet it would not have been a reality without the technological development. The industrialism in Europe flourished due to the colonialism as it provided the markets and the raw materials required for the industrial development. England, with the help of the trade, territory and the technology remained the leading economy of the World for about two hundred years.

The second technological revolution, which took place in the U.S. during last decades of the 19th century, provided a boost to the U.S. economy. The evolution of the internal-combustion engine, electric lights, telephone, telegraph, typewriter and the discovery of the petroleum were some of the technological developments of the time. Such revolutionary developments made the economy of the U.S. stronger which displaced that of England from the leading position in the World by the close of the 19th century.

The Economy of the industrialized world thereafter, passed through the 'long depression', which originated in Europe, during the later years of the 19th century. As a solution to the long depression, Colonial Empires were expanded, leaving almost no land in spare which could be colonized further. For swallowing up of Africa by the colonial powers of the day a conference was convened in 1884 in Berlin which was attended by the U.S. also.

In the beginning of the 20^{th}century, struggle for the global supremacy began between England and the United States. Sir Halford Mackinder, the British geo-political thinker and Parliamentarian, developed a theory of geo-politics in the support of the British supremacy but Germany tried to implement it to increase its power and influence in the affairs of the global significance.

After the World War First, the victorious Britain lost its economic supremacy to the hands of the U.S. when the British Pound Sterling was detached permanently from the gold standard on September 23, 1931, though the British Empire continued till the mid of the twentieth century.

Increasing production and decreasing sale of the industrial products along with stoppage of loans to the nations of Europe and Latin America by the U.S. were some of the causes of the 'Great Depression' of 1929. England was the first to recover from the depression with the help of the hidden resources of the Colonial Empire and de-valuation of British currency, the Pound Sterling.

The World War Second beginning in 1939, finally gave respite to the World from the great depression. New deal of Roosevelt F.D., the U.S. President, showed a ray of the hope in the U.S. society which was severely torn by the depression. The misery caused by the depression permeated in the life of the Americans which they had never seen before.

After World War Second de-colonization began and by the mid-1960s most of the nations of the World got independence from the colonial yoke, leaving behind the dismantled Colonial Empires. The mid-1960s is also remembered for the beginning of the de-industrialization in the U.S. and the emergence of the multi-national corporations in the field of the real economy.

The developed economies of the World faced the problem of the inflation and that of stagnation in the industrial development during 1970s which led the de-regulation, in the form of liberalization, privatization and globalization of the economy. The de-regulation and the supportive interventions of respective Governments boosted the industrialization in the nations of East-Asia.

The 1980s debt crisis in Latin America was caused by the imprudent Government decisions whereas the imprudent private sector and privatization led the debt crisis in the Asian nations during 1990s. The IMF and the World Bank applied the same policies in Asia which were executed in Latin America. The background and responsible factors were different in both the continents. The global financial and non-financial institutions did not play fairly and they were supposed to be one of the causes of the crisis in Asia.

The World saw the third Industrial Revolution in the form of the development of the information technology and communication system. The networking of computers revolutionized the information system globally. The 'internet', an international networking of the computers, changed the functional landscape of the World by close of the second millennium. The dot-com-boom of 1990s was the result of the expansion of 'internet' services.

The policy of the globalization, adopted during last decades of the 20th century, was built upon the debris of the neo-colonialism and it was the time of the beginning of the monopoly of the multinational corporations in the field of real economy. The production and productivity in the industrialized economies also got increased many fold. By the close of the 20th century, the gap between the rich and the poor widened and the gradually decreasing purchasing power of the masses went down below the critical limit by the beginning of the third millennium.

At the dawn of the 21st century China and India, the two highly populous and partial industrialized nations, appeared at the world-industrial-scene. Now the industrial landscape of the World includes the U.S. and Canada, Europe, Japan, East-Asia and parts of China, India, Russia and Brazil and other industrialized pockets elsewhere, with varying degree of the industrialization.

In the first decade of the 21st century, the burst of the dot-com-bubble and rise in the prices of the petroleum and other essential commodities including food material took place. The burst of the dot-com-bubble was followed by the formation of the real estate bubble and its burst was the result of the rise in the interest rate. Collapse of the prices of the real estate and the consequential foreclosure of mortgages in the U.S. were the other events.

The sub-prime crisis originated due to the rise of the interest rate in the U.S. and it became global because of the derivatives. Panic due to the crisis was felt almost everywhere and the market value of the stocks and the derivatives fell, leading to the reduction in the purchasing power of the masses. In the already fragile economic system the fall of the purchasing power created havoc and decelerated the momentum of the economic functions globally.

By the end of 2008, the crisis had engulfed whole of the global economy. It adversely affected almost every nation whether it was the small or the big, the developed or the developing. The developing nations were not concerned to the origin of the crisis but suffered much more. The developed economies where the problem originated were the first ones to be affected.

The crisis affected the Indian Economy like others but India succeeded in maintaining the economic growth at the rate of 6.5 percent in 2008-09 and 7.4 percent in 2009-10. The high growth in the crisis years was due to the demand created by the rural India and the agriculture. The crisis affected every sector of the Indian Economy but the most seriously affected ones were the export and the import and the ray of hope in the odd hours was the demand creation by the rural India.

The crisis has unveiled the weaknesses of the global economic system which have reached to an unsustainable level. In a sustainable economy the driving force comes from the real economy but it is far behind the financial one which is more developed and strong in the present world. Despite much development and strength the financial economy does not have capacity to carry the global economic system and it can not do so as it has not much employment generation capacity and covers a fewer people in its business.

The industrialized nations are retracting from the philosophy of the globalization in the time of the crisis, leaving the developing nations in the hot water. It is the time when global effort is required to get rid the problem off but the stronger and the richer nations are not only isolating themselves from the global efforts and concern which is required at the moment but are following the policies of the protectionism also.

The West under the leadership of the U.S. is pursuing the policy of the protectionism and it is blaming the globalization for the crisis. The era before the globalization was passing through the ideology of the neo-colonialism which was the reminiscent of the colonialism, the system which had brought industrialization and prosperity in the West on the cost of the East which was the colonial market at that time.

The question is whether the West is interested in the retrogression or the progression? Whether it is interested in bringing back the era of the colonialism or the neo-colonialism or interested in going ahead implementing the full-fledged globalization in all walks of the life?

The opportunistic behaviour of the West had compelled rest of the World in 1970s and 1980s to liberalize, privatize and open the economy. Such changes were required for the West but the East was not prepared to absorb the changes under which the economies were to be opened in the interest of the West. But when the globalization is required for the rest of the World, the West is going back from it leaving them in the troublesome situation.

The population of the World is a little less than 7 billion. The people reside in different nations on the earth but their views, ideas, thoughts, co-operation and representative participation are required for the sustainable development of the global economy which is growing larger in size and function. The champions of the democracy, the U.S., U.K. and so on have to consider the global public opinion. The attempts are being made to democratize the global institutions but every thing is happening half heartedly. The Luke-warm efforts are one of the causes of the present day problems.

The economic crisis has opened the eyes of the World to look at the roots of the present day problems. Going back would not be a solution but it would provide a psychological satisfaction of being protected in the crisis only. One of the solutions to the problems would be the full-fledged implementation of the concept of the globalization with the consent of the people of the World. It would be materialized through the Global Democratic Government, with the election of its members, directly from the people. It would give representation of the World in its governance and it would provide a platform for the global policy-making and solutions to the problems which are increasing day by day.

A little detailed description of the Economic Crisis 2008, which is still going on, is needed because it is the great divide in the world history and is the reckoning point for the changes and development of the future. Prelude of the crisis was paradoxical and oxymoronic. The industrialized world was busy in maximization of the profits with the investment in the real estate. The prices of the real estates were flying vertically and so were the prices in the stock and the capital markets, in the early years of the first decade of the first century of the third millennium.

The picture of the rest of the World was diagonally opposite, as the poor nations of the third world were suffering from the price-hike and the unprecedented food crisis. The food problem had already brought hundreds of millions of people below the extreme poverty line who were above it during the last decade of the twentieth century. With the emergence of the economic crisis, the food problem did not disappear rather it got relegated to the back seat, in the wake of the economic crisis 2008, 'the problem of the big'.

After rising in first few months, the prices of the petroleum and the food material started declining from June 2008, not because of any real change in demand and supply but due to the function of speculative forces. The financial instruments like derivatives etc. fell in terms of the value in the financial markets, after the beginning of the crisis.

One of the causes of the food price-rise which was followed by the economic crisis was the shortage of food material in absolute quantity because of the diversion of the food grain producing land into the land for farming of the crops required for bio-fuel and to be used for other non-agricultural purposes in the U.S. Other causes were the unfair distribution of the food material and more significantly the inability of the substantial population to buy it because of the consistent decline in the purchasing power of the masses.

The increased and the increasing income inequality had aggravated the food crisis significantly and it had been one of the reasons behind the declining per capita food in-take in countries like India and China before the economic crisis 2008. It is noticeable that the agricultural recession and the food crisis had been precursors of the 'Great Depression' of 1929.

In the U.S. and the West the burst of the dot-com-bubble in 2000 paved the path for the formation of the real estate bubble. The houses are not prerogative of a few but social promises to all. In the light of such a maxim the housing loans were disbursed to those who did not have job, assets and income. The houses were taken as mortgage for disbursing loans and it was called the sub-prime mortgage. The events which occurred simultaneously were the rise in petroleum prices that was already high as well as the sudden rise in the interest rate which were kept on low during the dot-com-boom period by the Federal Reserve of the U.S. followed by the decline of house-prices which very soon slumped to the floor.

In this background the mortgage default began which led to the foreclosure of the houses by the banks. The borrowers preferred foreclosure instead of repaying loan which was increased due to the rise in the interest rates. It was a purely mortgage-market crisis in the U.S. and it had nothing to do with the global economy.

What caused the crisis in the global economy was something else, about which none is talking. It was the derivative based on mortgages and mortgage-backed securities which created panic, fear, distrust and calamity in the global economy. Other than the derivative it was the leverage which played significant role in deepening the crisis.

Derivative, a very risky and complex financial instrument, is a natural corollary of the financial development. It was imperative for the regulators of derivatives to understand its limits, crossing which the risk increases many fold suddenly. The regulators needed to pay attention to how to deal with the derivatives but there was an apparent mismatch between the financial innovations and the ability of the regulators who could not assess the impact of derivative products which clouded the weaknesses of underlying transactions.

The sub-prime mortgages were securitized and derivatives were created over the mortgage-backed securities. The rating agencies deliberately and falsely certified derivatives as investment grade products. The financial institutions of the U.S. and Europe invested heavily in such derivatives.

Once doubts were created about the financial products like derivatives because of the default of the mortgages, they lost their glare and values and became worthless in the capital market. The assets value of the derivative-holders slumped down. A host of institutions, in different countries, got reduced their assets values, leading to the beginning of the crisis in the financial markets of the U.S. and Europe.

The highly leveraged financial institutions failed and fell in the trouble. The whole of the U.S. economy was highly leveraged and almost every segment of the U.S. society including household was a net borrower and leveraged. The net household-saving was negative but the investment was high. In general, investment comes either from savings and borrowings or from foreign investors. Asian saving was invested in the U.S. and Europe. The U.S. and European leverage needs attention by the regulators of the global economy to bring financial stability.

The collapsed financial institutions were Merrill Lynch, Lehman Brothers, Washington Mutual, Fannie Mae and Freddie Mac, American Insurance Group et.al. in the U.S. and Fortes etc. in Europe. The financial institutions collapsed because of the derivatives whereas the banks collapsed because of the over withdrawal within very short time due to the panic created by rumours.

The U.S. banks do not have Statutory Liquidity Ratio and Cash Reserve Ratio like the Indian ones. Hence, in contingent situation bank became bankrupt. In the 'Great Depression' of 1929, small banks had collapsed but in the on-going crisis the big banks collapsed in the U.S.

The direct impact of the financial crisis came on the institutions which were exposed to the derivatives and other volatile financial instruments. Such an exposure was the most in the U.S. and Europe and was less elsewhere. First and the foremost effect came in the stock-markets which fell sharply affecting not only the institutions but individuals also.

The individuals lost whatever they had and had invested in share-markets throughout the World. The net worth of the global capital reduced. Individuals' sufferings affected whole of the economic system adversely by reducing the purchasing power of the masses.

Investment dried up over the globe. The long-term capital investment was already low in the developing world; the short-term capital investment also got reduced sharply as the share-market was slumped. The foreign institutional investments were being disinvested and capital was being taken out of the developing world which put an additional pressure on the dollar demand and the share-market.

The firms of the developing world, for instance, the Indian firms were facing difficulty in raising funds abroad which was affecting the availability of dollars. Thus, investment and capital formation were reduced in the corporate sector. On portfolio, capital conversion from positive to negative flows led to a fall in the value of the currencies.

The reduced foreign investment was pressing domestic financial sector in the developing economies for additional credit. The financial system, after being affected by the crisis, finally led down the real economy, which is the bed-rock of the economic system.

The financial sector of the economy has no standing of its own. It derives its strength and resilience from the real economy. It is the real sector of the economy that drives the financial sector. The financial sector can not drive the real sector and the economy should be driven by the real sector not by the financial one.

Thus, in a healthy economic system the real economy should be stronger than the financial one which is not so, at present in the World. The size of the financial economy was about five times that of the real economy, at the time of the beginning of the crisis.

The economic growth, trade and manufacturing shrank in 2008 and are shrinking in 2009. Job-retrenchment and the unemployment increased. The trust and the confidence in the finance system evaporated. The decline in the trade was the largest in last 80 years, because of the burst of the credit-financed-consumer-boom in the West, created by the artificial stimulus of the speculative financial activity.

The American and the European imports declined, causing a systemic crisis in the merchandise and services exports from the rest of the World. Similarly the reduction in the global industrial production was again weathering the economy. The weathered economy was reflected in the decreasing opportunity of the jobs in the World.

The job-cut was the highest between September and November2008 and was 1.3 million, in the U.S. alone. The employees which were retrenched in December 2008 were 0.7 million and in February 2009 they were 0.65 million. The job loss was in tens of millions over the earth and is continued in 2009.

In February 2009, the unemployment rate was 8 percent whereas the teenager unemployment rate was above 20 percent in the U.S. In November 2008, there were 10.3 million people already jobless, other than retrenched ones in the U.S. Joblessness is the biggest worry in 2009 whereas it was crime and violence in 2007. The U.S. self-employment is in steep down turn in 2009. As the people are being laid-off the jobs, they would have less money to buy goods and services which means that even more people would lose jobs with no end in sight in 2009.

A smaller crisis, embedded in the bigger one was the credit-card crisis in the U.S. It affected more people than the housing crisis but amount involved in it was smaller. In the U.S. every one uses credit card, the joblessness would accentuate the problem as the jobless would be unable to repay the borrowed money from credit cards. The credit card debt grew from US$ 211 billion in 2002 to US$ 915 billion in 2007.

The industrialized nations were infusing liquidity in the market to save economy from the disintegration. The U.S. Government gave US$ 700 billion bailout to the financial system of the economy, for infusing liquidity in the market as banks after banks were collapsing in October 2008. But there was a long queue for bailout seekers like the U.S. home furnishing suppliers, Zoo keepers, Wine-growers, Funeral Directors, Landscape gardeners and so on.

Ironically, Obama Administration has become parochial in perspective from universalistic. It is protecting the American Economy by "growing bushes around the nation". In the time of crisis the U.S. has thrown the philosophy of globalization away. It has different ideologies for the peace and the crisis.

British Premier Brown has said that Britain was for the British. In the time of the crisis the European Union is not united, as there is no bailout for the European Union as a whole. The rich Western Europe is not willing to share with nations of the poor Eastern Europe. If the whites are not being spared in the time of the crisis what might be said about the grey and the black. That is, the Western World does have any programme for helping the developing world in the time of the crisis which has been advocate of the globalization when the third world was not prepared for it.

The economic crisis 2008 moves around trust and confidence. The Western World does not have the trust and the confidence in the policies having been pursued in the 21st century. Business leaders and political leaders don't trust each other. When business came into the problem and business leaders wanted recovery with the help of the political ones, they virtually denied saying that the business leaders are greedy and are incapable of dealing with business.

Similarly the bankers and the customers don't trust each other. The people of the West don't have trust in anyone whether they are pursuing the business, the finance or the politics. But all the three need people to run the system. Therefore, there is a need to restore the confidence and to build the trust in the system to recover from the crisis. The distrust has been created by widening inequality, corporate greed and the lack of suitable regulations.

Larry Elliot, the Guardian's Economic editor, wrote in the Guardian, re-published in 'The Hindu', an Indian daily news paper, on Tuesday, February 03, 2009, "what the new President identified was that the economic system of the past 30 years has been hugely- and unhealthily- skewed towards those at the top. In the U.S. workers were able to improve their living standard only by sending spouses out to work, working longer hours and double (sometimes triple) jobbing. Even when that was not enough, they borrowed more."

The question arises whether the economy was normal 30 years before i.e. in pre-globalization era? When did the skewness start in the economy? When was the economy normal?

To answer these questions retrospection of the history of the Modern World Economic System which began in 15th century is essential and useful.

2

Beginning of Modern Age

In the mid-15th century, the Greco-Roman Empire was limited to Constantinople, the city joining the Continents of Asia and Europe. Constantinople fell to the hands of Ottoman Turks in 1453 which is supposed to be the end of the Medieval Period and beginning of the Modern Age, the quickening of fresh life and energy in Europe. It was the end of the thousand years old Greco-Roman Empire. Turks went on spreading in Europe but were checked at the gate of Vienna. It is said that a Byzantine nobleman said in 1453 "better the turban of the Prophet than the tiara of the Pope."

Beginning of the Modern Age was the beginning of the new conflict in the European society. The conflict is not a new phenomenon for any society as it has ever been present in every society since the time immemorial with varying degrees. The new conflict was between the old feudal class and the new awakened middle one due to the exploitation of the masses by the feudal and the religious systems.

In the feudal system land was the wealth and for the newly awakened middle class the wealth was to be accumulated through the manufacturing and the trade. The conflict between the two continued for hundreds of years, thereafter middle class came in prominence in the Western Europe first. It was the time of breaking down of the old barriers which meant advancement in many directions such as in–science, art, literature, architecture and new discoveries. It is called renaissance, the birth of learning and art.

After 1453, Turks controlled the land and sea routes to the East which passed through Constantinople. The lure of gold from the East, the stories of Marco Polo and other travellers who had been in India and China excited the imagination of

Europe and drew many into the sea. The big merchants, traders and adventurers who wanted to get at the East tried to find out new ways of reaching the golden East. The maritime technological innovations played major role in sea-voyages, trade and discoveries of new territories in 16th century. In the course of the search for the East, the Europeans found a very vast land that was called –the continents of North and South Americas. Spain and Portugal established their Empires in Americas in the 16th century.

Spain conquered Grenada from the Arabs in 15th century and became the most powerful monarchy of Europe of the time. Spain and Portugal took the lead in the sea voyages, Spain went to the west and Portugal to the east. Christopher Columbus, with the help of the king Ferdinand and the queen Isabella of Spain and some of the private investors of Italy who had invested 50 percent of the cost of expedition, took the voyage in the west and reached the islands near present North America and called it 'India' and its people the Red Indian in 1492. Later on, the islands were called West Indies.

The two rivals for West Indies were Spain and Portugal. In 1493 'Bull of Demarcation' was issued by Pope and it was a North-South imaginary line, 100 League west of Azores Islands. Pope declared that Portugal was to have all Non-Christian lands to the east of the line and Spain to have all Non-Christian lands to the west of the line.

Portuguese Vasco-da-Gama moving in the east reached India via Cape of Good Hope, the southern tip of Africa. He arrived at Calicut, a famous port-city situated on the Malabar Coast of India, in 1498. The Portuguese reached Goa, a coastal region of the Western India, in 1510.

Cortes, the Spanish, conquered Aztec Empire of Mexico in 1519 and Pizarro ended the Inca Empire of Peru in 1530. The two old Empires of America along with their culture and civilization were ended forever.

In Spanish America, hordes of adventurers of Europe were eager for plunder and loot. Mexico and Peru were full of gold and silver which flowed to Spain unceasingly. With the wealth of the Spanish America Spain consolidated its position as the Supreme power of Europe of the day. The plundered gold and silver of Spanish America helped the Spanish people in the improvement of their consumption level.

The consumption level of Spain of that day could be compared with that of the U.S. of the present day. In both the situations imports came at the point of the consumption from all the directions. The U.S. consumption and imports steered the global economy before the crisis 2008. Similarly, the Spanish consumption and imports from England, Holland and other nations of Europe steered the European economy accelerating the circulation of the gold and the silver of Peru and Mexico throughout Europe.

In the first half of the 16th century the European trade became global under leadership of Spain and Portugal. The global trade of Europe was with Asia, Africa and Americas. The most of the capital involved in the trade and business came from the newly found and usurped territories of Spanish America mainly Mexico and Peru.

The trade and commerce of Europe gathered momentum from the gold and silver of Mexico and Peru, infused in the economies of Spain and Portugal. The economic system of Europe, developed around trade and commerce, was assisted from the outside in the form of the gold and silver of the Spanish America. Such an externally assisted economic system of Europe, especially of Spain, enhanced the purchasing power of the Spanish people, who could buy the goods coming to Spain from anywhere. It was the beginning of the prosperity of Europe in general and that Spain in particular on the cost of the silver and the gold of the Inca and the Aztec Empires of America. Europe not only enjoyed the prosperity but expanded territorially also, giving their people the two continents each bigger than Europe in boon. The American continents got colonized by the Europeans very soon.

The global development of the trade and the territorial expansion, over the American land, has been the crucial factor behind the beginning of the prosperity in Europe, under the leadership of Spain and Portugal. Spain was eager in establishing Empire, i.e., gaining territories whereas Portugal was interested in the trade and commerce. The Portuguese, to increase their trade and commerce, got spread themselves over the Asiatic nations on the coasts of the Pacific and the India Oceans including India in the East.

Plundering and territorial acquisition of Mexico and Peru had many monetary and financial consequences like rise in prices which occurred first in Spain and then followed the path of gold and silver in spreading other nations of Europe. In a century, the price rise was five folds in Andalusia and 250 percent in England.

Europe, through Portugal, was in regular trade connection with the East. China and India were then the prosperous countries in the East and were able to supply needs of Europe, viz. spices, clothes, metal products, artifacts and so on. The purchasing of goods in Asia and selling them in Europe was a big business.

Therefore, the gold and silver of the west (Spanish America) was invested in the trade with the East. The small and the medium businesses appeared and got spread in Europe which was an intra-continental business that infused the buying power in the European masses which gave boost to the inter-continental business too.

The Spanish and the Portuguese dominance remained short lived, almost hundred years throughout the 16th century but provided a sound footing, for further economic development of Europe. The newly gained territories liberated Europe of the population pressure as the Europeans got colonized themselves in the 'new found land' of Americas.

In the days of Emperor Charles-V of Spain, it was said that the Sun never sets on his Empire. Later on, the phrase was used for the British Empire which dethroned the Spanish

Empire. Pt. J.L. Nehru has written in 'Glimpses of World History' that almost contemporary ruler of India, Babar had described the Indian socio-economic picture of the time, in the Babarnama –"The chief excellence of Hindustan is that it is a large country and has abundance of gold and silver. Another convenience of Hindustan is that the workman of every profession and trade are innumerable and without end. For any work and any employment there is always a set ready, to which the same employment and trade have descended from father to son for ages''.

It was such a description that allured the Europeans to come India through any route, the sea or the land. The travelogues of Marco Polo and other travellers presented the similar picture of China and India of the medieval period when they were the prosperous countries in the World.

The World shrank, as the new discoveries came one after another and there was a little to discover, in 16th century. Portuguese Viceroy Albuquerque seized Malacca in 1511 and put to the end of the Muslim trade in the Arabian Sea. The Portuguese now controlled the trade of the spices and other eastern goods with Europe. They were basically the commercial people and did not attempt to develop colonies. They remained scattered and pursued business and trade and were the link between the East and the West.

In 1565, Spain expanded its colony occupying Philippines and sent soldiers and missionaries to the East. The Netherlands was under the Spanish rule and included Holland and a part of Belgium and its people were called the Dutch. After Emperor Charles-V, the Spanish Empire disintegrated. Spain and the Netherlands went to his son Philips-II.

The Dutch revolted against Spanish ruler Philips-II. The English privately helped the Dutch. Under the leadership of Drake, an English seaman, the Spanish treasure-ship from America was captured in the Atlantic Ocean. The war between Spain and England broke out. Dutch were already fighting with Spain. Portugal joined the war also. Spain had to fight with the Dutch, the English and the Portuguese at a time. With great deal of good luck and determination the English won the war. The 'Invincible Armada' sent by Spain to conquer England was wrecked in 1588.

Both, the victorious English and the Dutch invaded the Far East and attacked the Spaniards and the Portuguese. The Spaniards were all cantered in Philippines and succeeded in defending themselves as they had soldiers as well.

The Portuguese were scattered for the business purposes. That is why they could not defend themselves and lost the Eastern Empire and all that remained were a few small out-posts in India and elsewhere. Goa in Western India was the chief out-post of the Portuguese. They passed out of the Eastern history. The eastern trade now went to the hands of the Dutch and the English.

Gradually the Empire of Spain and the trade and commerce of Portugal faded away. But their role in the modern world history can not be dwarfed. They provided resources for the economic revolution in Europe. A new capitalistic group emerged from the peasantry and the middle income group in Europe, through the trade and the plundering from Americas and Asia, during the era of the Spanish and the Portuguese.

When Portugal was pioneering worldwide linkage to accomplish its trade interest overseas, the Dutch were intensifying trade relations between different parts of the Northern Europe. In 1570, the carrying capacity of the Dutch merchant shipping was almost equal to that of the combined fleet of England, France and Germany.

After 1588, the English and the Dutch got vast trade with the East. Both of them were highly interested in the trade of spices and silk from India, China and other parts of the East. England conquered most of the colonies of Spain and Portugal and laid the foundation of the British Empire.

In 1600, Queen Elizabeth gave a charter to the East India Company and in 1602 Dutch East India Company was formed.

The two companies were meant for the trade only. The English ultimately withdrew from Eastern islands and paid attention to India only whereas the Dutch continued their interest in Malaysia, Indonesia and so on.

In later half of the 17th century, there was a struggle for supremacy in Europe, in which Britain surpassed every one and emerged as the most powerful Imperial State in Europe. The Dutch lost all Asiatic territories except Indonesia to the English. The French also lost Asiatic and Caribbean assets to the English and were reduced to just a token colonial power. Brazil went out of the Portuguese hand. Spain lost its huge colonial empire in Latin America except Cuba and Puerto Rico and Philippines in Asia. England took over what the French and Dutch lost in Asia and Africa. It extended its trade and indulgence in India and started watching eagerly the political developments in India. It established a privileged commercial presence in Latin America too.

At the dawn of 18th century Spain, Portugal and Holland ceased to exist as major trading countries of Europe and the World. Now the conflict left was between the English and the French. In 18th Century India, North America and West Indies were the most valuable regions to trade with, far which the English and the French fought.

The French triangular trade was among Africa and West Indies and accounted for a quarter of the French trade by value. The French had extensive sugar-cane plantations in West Indies. The English triangular trade involved Africa and the Spanish-American colonies and returning cargo included sugar, cotton and tobacco.

In North America, Canada was in the French control, 13 colonies on the eastern coast were the English, the territory south of the 13 colonies was the Spanish and that in north-west was in control of the native people, the Iroquois Indians. The defeat of France by England in 1763, after 7 years war (1756-'63), ended the French-American Empire.

The Anglo-French War, fought in India, rooted out the French colonial ambition in India for ever, as the French were defeated by the English in the war in India too. England established the supremacy in the World commerce and trade. At that time, just before the industrial revolution, England had colonies in North America and West Indies prominently. India was in the making of a political dependency of England.

The English, the Spanish and the Portuguese carried on a cruel and heartless slave trade. Negroes, the native people of Africa, were captured and brought to Americas and West Indies for working in the plantation agriculture like tobacco, sugarcane etc. The prosperity of the southern part of the U.S. was dependent on the slaves, brought from Africa, before the abolition of the slavery in mid-19th century.

The slave trade formed a triangle. The trade originated from Europe where ships were loaded with the consumer goods and sailed to Africa where the commodities were sold. The poor inhabitants of Africa were caught like beast and loaded in ship and sailed to Latin America, West Indies and Southern North America to work in the fields of plantation crops like tea, coffee, sugarcane, tobacco etc. Then ships, loaded with gold and silver, used to go to Europe completing the triangle.

The non-agricultural secondary activities developed in England with the help of artisans from other European nations. The English learned cloth making from the Walloons of Belgium, silk-weaving from the Huguenots and the protestant refugees of France. Cottage industries were also developed in England, in which artisans worked in their own houses and in the smaller groups. London grew by thriving population of artisans, merchants and traders. As a result of the developing secondary economic activities, the per-capita income in England increased and was the highest among European countries.

The English supremacy in the beginning of the 18th century was based on improvements made in agriculture and financial economy with innovations of financial instruments followed by development in the trade and commerce. Earlier the English carried on trade with Africa of liquor and other consumer items. Their trade with the East was mainly of spices and silk. In 18th century the chauvinism and hegemony of England was established in the global trade and commerce.

In the mid-18th century, the most significant event in world history was the English control over India through East India Company. The Battle of Plassey in 1757, in which English were Victorious, changed the function of the East India Company. An exclusively trading company became the ruling and governing body of India. The governing was largely trading; trading was nothing short of plundering. Trade 'per-se' with India ceased to exist just after the Battle of Plassey in 1757. From that very day, virtually nothing came in India 'in lieu' of the Indian exports to England.

England had concentrated on India for hundreds of years and had left South-East Asian region for the Dutch. Later on, India was made a political dependency of England. But the industrial revolution which began after the invention of steam power by James Watt in 1765, made England dependent on India for the survival and growth of the British industries.

India was a political dependency of England whereas England was an economic dependency of India. Further economic development of England was solely dependent on India; because India was highly populous as well as Indians had purchasing power more than that of the people of other nations of Asia and Africa where English commanded hold. The North and South Americas and Caribbean Islands were colonized by the people of Europe and could not be exploited as the Indians could be.

The Industrial Revolution which began in England during last decades of the 18th century flourished because of the British Empire. India was the most important and useful colonial dependency so far as the English industrialization was concerned. Thus, industrialism developed, expanded and gave benefits to the English through the help of the capitalism, imperialism and geo-politics.

Geo-politics came into existence in 20th century when no space was left, on the earth, to be colonized by the colonial powers of the World. The European territorial expansion continued for about four centuries beginning from the early years of 16th century to the end of the 19th century. The true beneficiaries of the imperialism were England, France and the Netherlands; though it was started by Spain and Portugal and among them England was the highest gainer. After the Spanish Empire, it was the British Empire which never saw the sun-set in its territory.

By the end of the 18th century, South American nations were under Spain except Brazil which was under Portugal. In North America, Canada was under Britain. The 13 British colonies, of south-eastern part of North America situated on the coast of the Atlantic Ocean, had declared independence in 1776 by 'Declaration of Independence'.

The independent colonies were named as 'United States of America,' a new nation. It was the great republic of the modern age. The bitter civil war between the southern and the northern states resulted in the abolition of the slavery in mid-19th century. Development of the U.S. began in 19th century with massive European immigration and westward movement of production frontier with the help of the development of the railways, in second half of 19th century.

During the three centuries of economic revolution, beginning in 15th century, economic and administrative innovations occurred in North Western Europe. The most important of them were various new concepts, practices and institutions which governed the further financial economy of the World.

Development of the modern capitalist credit money facilitated exchange and investment across the market and region. New form of capital accounting was the result of monetary and banking innovations which gave new vistas in the capital accumulations. Systematic transfer of value and debt to the third party gradually depersonalized the negotiations between the strangers and made possible issuing of under-written bank money.

Money became able to be accumulated, stored and converted as a medium of financial exchange across the region and economic system. The joint investment in trading companies had already begun centuries ago. The world-extending-expeditions were funded by joint investment in Europe. The British East India Company and the Dutch East India Company had issued shares to the public to fund their expeditions.

The Bank of England was founded in 1694. In the same year government lotteries were re-established and remained a part of government finance between 1694 and 1826. Lottery tickets were the early government bonds. The ticket holders were entitled not only for a possible prize but for a periodic payment also. The Bank of England organized English State lotteries from 1710 onwards.

Insurance emerged as a result of the 'side bets on the outcome of draw' in a lively secondary market of lottery tickets. The trading sites were the "Coffee Houses" and one of them was converted into 'stock exchange' in 1773. Before the revolution of 1789, Paris was the financial centre of the Imperial World. Thereafter, London replaced Paris as a centre of finance.

Theory of the mercantilism, prevailing in the era of the Economic Revolution, was to promote the economic interests of its country by encouraging and protecting foreign trade, the most effective method of increasing national wealth. Earlier the most effective way to increase national wealth was to accumulate gold and silver.

In 17th century, when the English and the Dutch replaced the Spaniards and the Portuguese, the means of accumulation of national wealth changed. Now, the means of the accumulation of the wealth became importing raw material and exporting manufactured goods.

To ensure the conditions favourable to the pattern of the trade and accumulation of the wealth, the supply of the raw material and the markets for the manufactured goods had to be assured. There was a competition among the colonizers for the raw material and the markets of foreign countries. The prevailing economic theory favoured establishment of the Colonial Empire which was to provide raw materials and captive markets for the industrially produced goods in the 'mother' country.

It was the era of the making of the economically self-sufficient Empire. The colonies were the commercial undertakings. Thus, the European nations were economically dependent on the colonies. The colonies were bases of the economic development of 'mother' countries in Europe. In absence of the colonies, countries of Europe would not have developed as fast as they developed or would have other stories.

The initiatives taken by Spain and Portugal were bases for developing trade links between far-off regions. The Dutch were linking India and Indonesia in the Far East and North and South Americas in the Far West to Europe. The Dutch were soon challenged by the English and the French. The English eliminated Dutch hold over international shipping. There was military conflict between the Dutch and the English between 1652 and 1674. The English won and established the supremacy in the trade with India and beyond.

Hartshorne and Alexander have vividly described the mercantilist international trade in the book titled 'Economic Geography'. A glimpse of it is as follows:

"Lekachman writes "mercantilists believed that the gain of one country was inevitably the loss of another. If this is true the case, some would argue that the tremendous amount of economic benefit Europe derived from mercantilist trade came at the expense of many of today's under developed countries of Africa, Asia and Latin America. No matter how one interprets this phase of world economic history, the fact remains that mercantilist international trade contributed tremendously to thrust Western Europe into the process of dynamic and accelerated economic development by the end of 1750."

The Economic Revolution has played decisive role in the development and the modernization of Europe. It had revolutionized the economic activities of the day. Leaving behind the traditional system, non-agricultural secondary economic activities evolved and flourished in Europe. A web of hierarchical system of trade and commerce evolved in Europe with global connections including intra-national, national, international, intra-continental and inter-continental trade.

The Western Europe exploited the American resources, on which its further economic development took place. The exploitation of agricultural resources could be possible by slaves, traded from Africa. The local American people could not withstand the European diseases, gone with colonizers, like small pox and most of them died of and remaining relegated in the deep forest. During the slave trade era almost 30 million people were traded to Americas and Caribbean from Africa.

In Europe, mercantilism replaced the feudal production structure and the most important activity became "commercial production of goods." The new economic activities were centred on the towns and small cities. The growth of the cities, in number and size, accelerated.

The surplus production began which led to the buying and selling at commercial level. The era witnessed, buying and selling of the land, labour and capital as a commodity in the market too. The economic activities expanded rapidly. Cities became centre of production and an economic hinge of the mercantilism.

The domestic economic activities played crucial role in the accumulation of the capital and in dynamic economic growth of the Western Europe. The dynamism in domestic economic activities was not internally boosted rather it was boosted from the outside in the form of the profits and other gains from the mercantile as well as slave trades.

The impact of the slave trade on African economy was disastrous, as it created severe shortage of the labour-force, due to deployment of the youth, in the form of slaves, hampering agricultural processes and disrupting other domestic production activities, inhibiting Africa's socio-cultural and economic development.

A new group of earning more and doing nothing evolved in Europe. It was the group of investors in imperial expeditions, for instance, in 1492 investment was made by merchants of Italy in Columbus' expedition. Investments were made in companies. The investors in East India Company used to get dividend 100 percent, 150 percent even up to 200 percent annually.

The share-markets evolved to make the investment for maximization of the profits. The lottery tickets were sold and purchased, even bet on the possible out-come of draw of lottery tickets was in practice. It was a sizeable group, affluent, doing nothing and making profit.

The economy of the period was properly divided into financial and real economies. The real economy was the prominent in comparison to the financial one. Trade was the most important economic activity. During the era of the economic revolution, England was the liquor seller in Africa along with cotton clothes and some other manufactured goods.

Before the industrial revolution England had captured both the triangular trade systems. The triangle consisting of Europe, Africa and Latin America was already in the English possession and triangle formed by Europe, Africa and West Indies came in the English hand which was earlier in the French control.

3

Industrial Revolution and Long Depression

A few significant mechanical inventions, of the early years of the 18th century, were the precursors of the Industrial Revolution in England. The flying shuttle for cloth-weaving made by Kay in 1738 brought tremendous change in the method of the cloth-weaving. As a result of the use of the flying shuttle the cottage and the small scale industries gave way to the mechanized-large-scale-commercial production in the field of the cotton industry. Another significant mechanical invention was the spinning jenny of Hargreaves in 1764.

Before the invention of the steam-power by James Watt in 1765, the machines were driven by the water power. Later on, using the steam-power the steam-engine was designed, fabricated and used in the factory to drive the machines. The coal, a source of the power, was used to produce steam to be used in the steam-engine. Therefore, the coal-industry developed as a by-product of the development of the steam-engine and its large scale commercial use in the industries. The new factories driven by the steam power swallowed up many of the cottage industries.

The inventors of the new innovations were born in middle class, the worker class, not in the elite class but the benefits of inventions were reaped by the elite and business classes whose views regarding labourers were quite inhumane as Pt. Nehru has depicted in his 'Glimpses of World History'–"The governing class developed quite a convenient philosophy that the poor were necessary for society and therefore, it was quite virtuous to pay low wages. If higher wages were paid the poor would try to have a good time and would not work hard enough."

The factory owners developed a new philosophy which was called 'laissez-faire', i.e., they did what they liked in their business without any interference from the Government. The capitalistic mode of production gained maturity after the Industrial Revolution which was started and nourished in the era of the Economic Revolution. Afterwards, the production technology and the capital became central in the production processes and in the industries.

Textile industry was the first to be affected by changes in the production technology. In the field of transportation the steam-ship came first and reduced the distance in terms of time. The cost of transportation was also reduced. Consequently, the range and the area of the distribution of the industrially produced goods increased. The industrial production capacity expanded because of the increased accessibility to the raw material and the natural resources. The steam-ship facilitated the transportation of the raw materials from far-off regions like India and Latin America on the regular and the sustained basis.

Coal was the only source of the power for the steam powered machines. Coal-mining developed in Britain first and then exploration of the coal started elsewhere including India. Jharia and other coal mines of India were explored and exploited in the interest of the British industries.

Iron and Steel industry followed the cotton and the coal with the beginning of the smelting of the pig iron in England. With the development of the technology, the manufacturing of the steel was begun. Initial use of the steel was in the ship-building which enhanced the naval power of England. The ship and shipyard contributed to the development of harbours which directly improved the international trade of England.

Near about 1830 Stephenson's famous engine the 'Socket' came into the existence which laid the foundation of the railways. Thus, the steam-powered rail came into the existence. With the development of the iron and steel industry, railway lines were first laid down in England to join the cities then elsewhere in Europe, Americas and other parts of the British Empire to exploit the raw material and the captive markets. As a result of Industrial Revolution, manufacturing superseded the agriculture as an economic activity and became the primary source of the livelihood in England.

England: An Economic Dependency of India

Before onset of the Industrial Revolution in England, India was in the way to be made the English dependency. In India, the Battle of Plassey in 1757 was won by East India Company. From that very day the trade of East India Company with India ceased to exist. What began thereafter was nothing short of plundering, under leadership of Lord Clive. The money, extorted out of India provided a booster to the starting of new industries of cotton textile in Manchester industrial region of England which was in the process of the development during the last decades of 18th century.

Industrialization is an expensive process, in beginning it swallows up money without return for sometime which is a gestation period. The gestation period of the mechanized industries is longer than that of the small and the cottage industries. India provided the required vast sum of the money along with the raw material, the cotton as well as the market for the British industrially produced clothes.

The Indian market was not easily accessible to the English as India had already developed cotton industry. The English had to adopt all devices to ruin the Indian industries. Britain forced India to be fit in the British Scheme of the industrialization.

The capitalists, who had earned money through shares in different companies trading with the East like East India Company or with the West in the triangular circuits involving slave trade with Africa and Americas, established industries first in England.

With the industrialization, the capitalism led to a new type of imperialism which searched everywhere raw materials and markets. In such circumstances, Britain tightened colonial clutches over India and started squeezing the Indian raw materials and markets swiftly. The political hold was essential to achieve such an imperial objective and India became a political dependency of England for an economic reason too.

The textile industry of England was the first to be developed, with the arrival of new technology and machines, in the later years of the 18th century. During the period from 1780 to 1840 the cotton was the main industry and England was the only industrialized nation in the World.

The industrial development of England was based on the core-periphery model, in which peripheral economies were made dependent on the core economy but reality was something else. The industrial development and food security of the core-economy depended primarily on the raw-materials, food materials and markets of the peripheral economies.

There was a bloody struggle for the peripheral economies amongst the industrially developing economies of Europe. In such a struggle, England had edge over others because of the initial lead in the industry and colonial expansion. England had dependencies like India where half of the total cotton exports of Britain could be forced to absorb. In the first quarter of 19th century the cotton products constituted half of the English exports.

The second phase of the English industrialization was based on the steel manufacturing and it began around 1840. The steel products were mainly consumed in the ship-building and railways. It was the era when the English capitalists invested capital in the railways throughout the English Empire and Americas. The era experienced the railway boom. In the investment of railways the largest share went to India, the U.S. and Latin America. The investors had accumulated the wealth through fair and unfair means adopted in different forms of trade and exchange from India and other parts of the Empire.

United States of America

The first English permanent settlement at American Continent was built at Jamestown of Virginia by a small band of settlers in 1607. It was purely a business venture and the settlers earned benefits from trapping and trading in fur. The colonies grew in number and size and became thirteen in number. In due course of the time, middle class emerged in the 13-British-Colonies, crying for 'unalienable rights of life, liberty and property', a phrase borrowed from John Locke's Second Treatise on 'Civil Government' published in 1690.

By 1770, the Thirteen British Colonies were ready for self-government movement. The colonies declared independence making a new nation 'United States of America' in 1776. The U.S. Constitution was adopted in 1787, making entire nation a unified and common market formed by the Thirteen British-Colonies. It was a small independent farming economy by the close of the 18th century.

From the beginning of 19th century, the U.S. economy started expanding and developing on its own. Jeffersonian democracy came into prominence after 1801 when Jefferson became the President of the U.S. whose view was to protect the common man from the political and economic tyranny. For him, the small farmers were the most valuable citizens of the U.S. and he protected them.

The agrarian economy moved towards the commercialism with giving primacy to the cotton and other plantation crops supported by the slaves in south. It was the beginning of inequality in the U.S. society as some families became very wealthy because of the slave labour and plantation farming.

A country with thirteen colonies, on the coast of the Atlantic Ocean, expanded gradually as the settlers from Europe continued to arrive. The present boundary of the U.S. except Alaska and Hawaii was achieved by 1853. In the territorial expansion of the U.S., transportation links played a major role.

The Government created national roads and water ways. Roads, canals and harbours were built by Clay's American system supported by Whig Party. It protected industry and created strong national banks. Railways contributed much more in the development of the U.S. economy.

At that time England was overflowing with the wealth and capital. The profits earned from India and other parts of the British Empire were invested in the development of the U.S. railways. The railways linked far-off regions of America and gave the nation a continental size in economy and polity both.

With the development of transportation system new markets opened in different parts of the nation and vast regions in new territory developed. The European investment and national commitment was the backbone in the development of the large-scale railway system which paved the path for the country's all round development and industrialization.

The Industrial Revolution, begun in Europe in 18th century, was started in the U.S. in early 19th century and transformed the country from the agrarian to the industrial economy. Economic History of the United States, from Wikipedia, the free encyclopedia, presents a picture of the U.S. of 19th century in the following words:

"By mid-19th century, the U.S. had surpassed Tsarist Russia, Revolutionary Prussia and almost matched France and India in purchasing power though sea trade routes were dominated by the Royal Navy's gunboat diplomacy...By the late 1880s; the U.S. had overtaken the U.K. as the World's most powerful economy."

During the last decades of the 19th century, the U.S. went through "Second Industrial Revolution" which included the discovery of petroleum in Western Pennsylvania and invention of petrol and diesel-driven internal-combustion engines. Other inventions of the time were telephone, phonograph, telegraph, type-writer, electric light and so on.

The new discoveries and inventions brought profound changes in the economy and the society of the U.S. With technological development, the U.S. economy in new form and feature developed in leaps and bounds. A new conflict arose between the traditional British economy and the techno-based modern economy of the U.S. by the beginning of the twentieth century.

The Long Depression

During the first 70 years of 19th century, a variety of industries developed in Europe and the U.S. England remained politically and economically the most significant nation in the core economies and its industrial products were sold across the globe. The industrial production and capacity to produce were increased much more in the core economies.

The British capital, invested in the most parts of the World, was in the process of the maximization. England was overflowing with surplus capital and there was shortage of the space to invest it to maximize the benefits in the second half of 19th century.

John Stuart Mill, leading economist of England, has described problems of capital glut resulting from the creation and the accumulation of far more industrial and financial capital than could be utilized. The result was the decrease in industrial capital productivity and financial capital remained idle just kept in banks not in circulation. Consequently, the margin of profit began to decline as there was stagnation in the development of the technology.

After 1870, the industrially advanced British economy, encountered the problems regarding the international trade, sustained economic growth and the excess capital. It broke the 19th century peaceful growth in the economies of core countries. Other than England, the U.S., Germany, France, Austria, Czarist Russia were interrupted on the stage of the economic development. The main competitors of Britain were the U.S., France and Germany.

In Germany, new enterprises like Deutsche Bank were founded and the war reparations achieved from France encouraged the stock-market speculations. The shares and stocks were from the railways, factories, docks, steamships etc., the areas where the development was taking place in Germany, the U.S. and other nations of Western Europe.

In Vienna, Berlin, Paris, London, St. Petersburg and New York share-markets came down in 1873, causing depression in the core economies which lasted in some form for about 23 years, i.e., up to 1896. The depression withheld the development of Europe and America, reduced the profit and checked the trade and commerce.

The European powers tried to solve the problem of depression in the old manner, through the expansion of the colonial markets. The development of the newly industrialized nations like the U.S., France and Germany virtually forced England to protect its colonial markets and resource-base, as they had begun to compete for markets, raw materials and the natural resources.

To save its superiority and supremacy in the global economy, England pursued imperialism and colonialism more aggressively. England had made its trade global with removing all trade and tariff restrictions unilaterally. Free trade of Britain was imposed on the colonies, dependencies like India, protectorates, directly ruled states and other parts of formal and informal British Empire.

China, Persia, Thailand and Ottoman Empire were not within the formal Empire of England but they were part of informal Empire and did not have sovereignty in the economic and commercial matters. There were treaties between these nations and England which granted England extra-territorial rights. Under the treaties, these nations had to maintain low tariff for the British goods.

During last decades of the 19th century, Britain found that the available territory was not sufficient to satisfy the industrial greed of the British capitalists. It used its powerful naval forces to annex the territory found anywhere. Most of the territories were annexed from Polynesia during this period. The imperial annexation of land provided extra markets for

Britain, to maintain high level of profit by selling its industrial products in 'the new lands'.

If expansion of Empire was the solution to the economic slowdown or decline in marginal profit then it was available not only to England but also to other colonial powers including the U.S. There was a tug-of-war for the African territory amongst different powers of Europe like Britain, France, Germany and others. But their long-term interest was not to be served by fighting each other for the territories.

By 1875, only Africa and Polynesia had sufficient land unconquered by the Europeans. In November 1884, 'Berlin Conference' of the colonizers was convened in the leadership of German Imperial Chancellor Otto Von Bismarck to slice out the African land to satisfy the imperial greed and to suck the blood of already naked, hungry, bloodless, exploited as slaves for the centuries. The lion's share of the African territory went to the French and the English. It was attended by the U.S. also.

When the Africans could not be sold as slaves they were compelled to leave their sovereignty and they were forced to purchase which they did not need. Even after the division of the African territory amongst the colonial powers their greed was not satisfied. They further stiffened and deepened the colonial control and extended it in the Middle-East and Asia, as the colonialism was the economically beneficial pursuit for the colonizers.

With the Industrial Revolution, a new economic pattern, called the core-periphery model, evolved in the global economy, in which the core economies were dependent on the peripheral ones for the raw material and the markets. The model illustrates the dependency relation amongst the nations as well as the selective industrialization in the industrial landscape of the World.

England and other emerging industrial nations of the Western Europe and the U.S. had accumulated the excess capital during the course of the industrial development. Economist John Stuart Mill had pointed out that the resource-rich territories of the peripheral economies of Africa, Asia, Latin America and other parts of the World were "guaranteed productive outlets" for the excess capital generated in the industrial countries of the core-economy.

The guaranteed access to the raw material and markets for the European products was essential for the sustenance of the process of industrial development. Europe needed a large consumptive market for its industrially produced goods. The Europeans were distributed in three continents, namely North America, South America and Australia and New Zealand. They were producers in most of the cases than consumers of the products of the European industries.

Before colonization, the Europeans did not have high aristocratic life style in consumption. The newly developed aristocratic consumption pattern was supported by colonies. For instance, the silk and porcelain from China, tea and spice from India, gold, diamond and ivory from Africa and sugar from Latin America and West Indies were the special commodities consumed in Europe which were available at minimal prices due to the colonialism.

The European domestic problems were also resolved through the colonialism which was a safety valve for the European out-cries. The domestic unemployed and underemployed people were sent to work in the colonies. The industrial workers' conditions and the standard of living of the people in Europe improved only after the increased exploitation of the colonies. Thus, colonialism brought prosperity and high living standard in Europe on the cost of the colonial people. With the development of industries, agriculture relegated to the back seat and became secondary source of the livelihood in Europe. In this background, colonies became main suppliers of the food-material for the colonial powers. The food supply from colonies kept the cost of food-material and inflation low. Consequently, the wages were kept at lower rates in Europe which increased the profits of the industrialists.

4

Early Years of the Twentieth Century

The late 19th century colonial expansion of markets enabled economy of the World to resurrect again in 1890s. The revival of the European economy was more dependent on the colonial expansion than anything else whereas that of the U.S. was mainly supported by the new technological advances like arrival of internal-combustion engine, electricity and so on.

The U.S. and the German economies soon surpassed the British one in terms of the production volume. The industrial development in both the countries was endogenous based on their national and natural resources and technological advancements. By turn of the 19th century, the main economic powers in the World were the U.S., Germany and Britain.

By then, barring a few 'unproductive' patches, whole of the earth was occupied by the colonial powers. Imperialism was at the height; only might was right, nothing else. When nothing was left to be colonized, the big imperial powers tried to subdue or subordinate smaller imperial powers. It was the beginning of the manifestation of the cut-throat struggle amongst the colonial powers.

The early years of the twentieth century saw the play of the powers based on the principle of 'matsya nyay', big fish eats the smaller ones which gave birth to a new science called geo-politics. The concepts and the practices of the new science provided theoretical platform for the struggle on the global territorial space to establish the supremacy and control over the resources of the World.

The first geo-political theory was presented by English geographical thinker and Parliamentarian Sir Halford Mackinder before Royal Geographical Society of London in his paper entitled "The Geographical Pivot of History" in

1904. The other important geo-political theorists were Karl Haushofer, a German scholar, Spykman, an American thinker and et al. The three scholars reached on the entirely different conclusions and policy formulations, working-out from the similar historical and geographical premises, because of the different vantage points.

The geo-political theory is not an objective but highly subjective entity. From Mackinder's vantage point his theory was meant for the perpetuation of the British hold over the world economy and polity which was threatened. The apparent threat to the British supremacy was from the emergence of Germany as an economically strong nation based on its own resources.

The emergence of the U.S., a continental-sized economy in itself and the Second Industrial Revolution which had taken place in it had shaken the confidence of Britain. The British liberal international economy based on unrestricted market and free trade was shaking. In this threatened situation, the British industries needed protection from the free trade policy of its own which permitted the unrestricted entry of the foreign industrially produced goods. The U.S. and Germany were posing threat to the British supremacy.

In this background, Mackinder tried to present a geographical and historical rationalization of the British supremacy. No single country seemed to pose a threat to Britain. Therefore, England was to prevent any alliance between Germany and Russia which might have threatened the leadership of Britain as Russia had vast area of continental size with strong resource base.

Theory also aimed to provide a vision and an insight to the British foreign policy which needed reforms desperately. The politico-economic scenario was changing. The colonial expansion was almost over but the struggle for the colonial re-distribution was emerged. The vast British Empire was not pleasant to other colonial powers.

The basic idea behind the German geo-politics was

Mackinder's Theory. Hausofer himself was magically attracted by Mackinder's paper titled "The Geographical Pivot of History" presented in 1904. The German scholars believed that State was an expanding spatial organism and expands on the cost of the neighbouring States.

The Germans wanted a larger living space or empire so they tried to gain control over the Eastern Europe. Other logical step leading to a German dominated world was to be accomplished through a treaty of mutual friendship with Russia. The German objective was to be achieved by the theory of Mackinder which had given a maxim-

"Who rules Eastern Europe commands the Heartland;
Who rules the Heartland commands the World-Island;
Who rules the World-Island commands the World."

(*Mackinder, 1919*)

For Mackinder "heartland" was a region stretching from the river Volga in the west to eastern Siberia in the east and from the Himalayas and related mountains in south to the Arctic in the north. This region was surrounded by the mountain barriers on the three sides and an ice-bound sea on the fourth and which was not accessible to sea powers but was vulnerable to land forces in the south-west, through the Eastern Europe, between the Ural mountain and the Caspian Sea, a narrow corridor covered by the steppe grasslands. 'World Island' as referred here is huge united landmass of Europe, Asia and Africa.

The theory became guiding principle of Germany after 1919 and to some extent made contribution in the Second World War as Germany tried to have control over Eastern Europe. It provided a theoretical foundation for the global territorial struggle which was surfaced due to the unequal development in Europe, taken place during the period of the industrialization. One of the reasons behind the skewed development was the unequal sizes of the colonial empires which affected the factors of the industrialization like the sources of raw materials and the markets.

The failure of the idea of the equalization of the colonial empire amongst the major colonial powers of Europe gave rise to the formation of new alliances and the armament race. Germany, which did not have proper share in the colonies, according to its need and desire, for becoming the world power, followed the theory deeply.

V.I. Lenin presented an imperial analysis of the economic relations among the nations of the World in 1916. It was basically an analysis of the core-periphery relation, that is, the relation between the nations of the core and that of the periphery in comparison to the relation among the nations of the core and that of the periphery.

He concluded that the colonial expansions were the bone of contention amongst the colonial powers which aggravated the rivalry to the extent of the World War, which was nothing but the clashes of the imperial interests of the imperial powers. The colonies were economically very useful for well-being of the people of the colonizers mainly the European Nations. They permitted higher wages, better living conditions and reduced revolutionary fervour in the working community of Europe and America on the cost of the colonies in the peripheral nations.

The huge profits were derived from the colonial economic pattern, based on core-periphery model. The model envisaged that the nations of the core were the producers and industrially advanced and those of the periphery were consumers and suppliers of the raw materials due to the industrial backwardness.

The colonialism strengthened the exploitation and deteriorated living conditions in the Empires. At the same time, it generated a new revolutionary fervour in the down-trodden masses of the Empire, on which whole of the capital economy of the colonizers depended. In this way, an international class- struggle was generated between the 'haves' and the 'have-nots'.

Erstwhile USSR

The invention and the construction of the rail engine affected more the continental sized countries like the U.S. and Russia than the smaller ones. Social changes in Russia were accelerated by the construction of the railway between St. Petersburg and Moscow in second half of the 19th century. The construction of railways in Russia completed with that of between St. Petersburg, in the west and Vladivostok, situated on the Pacific coast, in the east, in 1903.

On account of the defeat of USSR by Japan in 1905 and heavy losses incurred during the World War First, social discontent increased and went beyond the critical limit. The Bolsheviks, a faction of the Soviet Democratic Party, took over the governance, through a revolution, in November 1917. It is called 'October Revolution' because in old calendar it was the month of October.

After the revolution, the power went in the hands of communists, who wanted to make Russia a class-less egalitarian society developed around the communes. The country became Union of Soviet Socialist Republic (USSR), the first Communist State developed on the debris of the World's largest monarchy. 'October Revolution' was the urbane in nature because it was supported by the factory workers of St. Petersburg and the military.

Industrialization of Russia was begun long ago but 1913 is taken as the reference year when the textile and the food processing industries were started. Lenin introduced new economic policies which made semi-capitalistic arrangements in USSR, in 1921-22. It restored the "limited free market economic pattern" where peasants were permitted to sell the produce of their land which was earlier forcefully taken.

The economy recovered swiftly but Lenin died in 1924, Joseph Stalin followed him who introduced the policy of industrialization through the national planning. The comprehensive development programmes were implemented, in the form of Five Year Plans, from 1928. The emphasis of the National Plans was on the collectivization of agriculture, heavy manufacturing industry and electrification. The socialized economy expanded until the World War Second, when Germany destroyed the developments made in USSR.

During the 4th Five-Year Plan (1946-50), the war-torn-ruined economy of USSR was rebuilt but Stalin died in 1953. Nikita Khrushchev followed him but he was dethroned when economic growth slowed down. Leonid Brezhnev followed him in 1964 and brought changes in the international policies of the trade and foreign relations. Agriculture was revitalized with the introduction of fertilizers, irrigation and machines. The collectivization of farmland provided surplus capital for the industrialization.

Iron and Steel and metallurgy industries were well developed since long. Machine building, machine tools, metal fabricating industries developed in the planning era. All round and full swing manufacturing and economic development took place in USSR under the planned economy. During 1980s, with the involvement in the world political and economic affairs, opening of the country to the atmosphere of the World began. The western consumerism expanded in the country. In 1991, it disintegrated into 15 independent states which formed Commonwealth of Independent States.

World War Frst is the most important event in the early years of the twentieth century and its significant impact was on the U.S. and Britain. The British supremacy in the World and its economic bases dwindled whereas the U.S. emerged stronger, after the World War First. Before the War, the U.S. was indebted to Britain and after it almost every nation of the World became debtor to the U.S.

The U.S. was following policy of the selective protectionism and was unwilling to the inflow of the foreign goods. It had acquired such a position that it could bring down economy of any country just by stopping further lending. The ourrencies of the poor countries were on the mercy of the U.S. and its wishes as well as it could bring crash in economy of any country during 1920s.

In the pre-war period Britain followed the free-trade policy but after the War situation was changed and the pre-war policy was hampering the interests of Britain as the U.S., Germany and France had become economically stronger and were supplying the goods in the markets of Britain and its Empire.

In the post-war period whole of the Europe was broken and ruined. The world-view of the Europeans was narrowed down and they had started thinking in terms of the nation instead of the inter-nation. The colonial powers followed the policies of the economic nationalism, in which foreign goods were kept away by implementing various devices like imposition of the heavy duty and tariff. The other aspect of the policy of nationalism was a slogan- 'buy home-made goods' which damaged the international trade heavily.

Europe was in trouble, individual nations were protecting themselves but their lust and the desire for the colonial and imperial exploitation was not softened rather was intensified. The concept of humanism was evolved in Europe but the colonial people were far away from being treated as human beings, perhaps human beings lived in Europe only.

The already existing cleavages in the polarized world widened due to the greed of the colonial exploitation. The emerging economies of Europe wanted redistribution of the colonies as they were the bases of the economic development and prosperity of the colonizers. The widening cleavages resulted in the outbreak of the World War Second.

The European nations were reduced to the status of indebtedness internally and externally both. Externally they were indebted to the U.S. and that was to be paid in gold whereas internal loans were to be paid in their national currency notes.

The paper currency is a fiat money and performs its function of credit. The paper currency is printed against certain reserves like gold, silver and foreign currencies. Printing and issuing of currency notes, without regard of backing reserves of the currency notes, kept in Central Bank of a nation, the credit and value of the printed and issued currency note is bound to fall. The fall of value and credit of the currency is the rise of inflation.

Printing currency is not the creation of the money but it is the creation of the credit against the backing reserves kept in the Central Bank of a nation. The inflation is indicator of the credit of the currency, the Central Bank of a nation and the Government issuing the currency. The inflation is inversely proportional to credit of currency, Central Bank of a nation and the Government issuing the currency, i.e., high inflation indicates low credit of the currency, the Central Bank and the Government.

One of the attempts made in different nations to solve the internal loans was the use of the concept of inflation. During 1922-23 Germany used the concept of the inflation to settle the internal loans. The Deutsch Marks, the currency notes, were printed ignoring the backing reserves of gold, silver and foreign reserves kept in the Central Bank of Germany; therefore, inflation rose very high in Germany.

Inflation affects creditor adversely. The Government was debtor and public was creditor and with the inflated money the Government settled its internal loans. In the process public suffered as it got inflated money which had less purchasing power. The Government made clean sweep of the savings of middle class whose savings got evaporated as they got inflated money in lieu of their bonds etc. The Government returned again to a stable currency system.

The tug-of-war between the U.S. and Britain began during the World War First when England was not in a position to make repayment of £ 50 million to the U.S. in 1917. During 1920s, the American trade expanded on the cost of that of England and Germany and equalled to that of England.

The U.S. accumulated the World's two third gold and enormous amount of foreign Governments' stocks. London lost its hundreds of years old seat of power and prestige despite the great victory of England in the World War First.

Throughout the 19th century, London had been the seat of the world finance, international exchange and politics. The exchange business has been a profitable business in England, for which it used to get tributes from all parts of the World and it was done by bank of England.

In international trade the payments were made through auxiliary money and credit papers like cheques or bills of exchange along with gold. In the situation of short of bills of exchange, the payment could be made in well-known securities, the Government bonds, loans or shares of international companies.

Under the gold standard system where value of national currency was fixed in terms of gold, anyone could demand payment in terms of gold. Different national currencies were stable and international trade grew up to the World War First. Then the system broke and economies became unstable and so became the currencies, except the dollar of the U.S.

After the end of the World War First positions of England and the U.S. changed. New York was all set to take the financial position of London. The inevitable conflict between the bankers of London and New York arose. The American pressure shook the English pound. Now pound was falling and varying as it was no longer pegged to the gold standard and England was unable to deliver gold on its currency.

During 1926-27, value of the French currency fell and settled on 20 percent of its previous value. After 1927, the French sold foreign securities and foreign bills of exchange to the Government as they got five times more money.

During 1920s, almost all the currencies fell which remained as firm as the rock of Gibraltar was the U.S. Dollar. England, to get the American friendship, to which it needed, gave up its Japanese alliance but England was not prepared to give up its financial leadership.

It was the 'financial leadership' which the U.S. wanted, for which the bankers, supported by both the Governments, fought. The American bankers opened branches and agencies world-wide and took the help of the French, the Swiss and the Dutch Bankers against London to organize traffic of foreign bills of exchange but did not get much success against the English experience of long and good play.

After 1924, when the German Dutsch Mark was stabilized and the capital was returning to the German banks, Germany returned to the U.S. bloc. The U.S. got a variety of bills of exchange because of the entry of Germany in its bloc.

In 1925, Britain came back on the gold standard to bring back exchange business in London which had been very much important in the past. The gold standard and the stable exchange rate of the currency benefited bankers and creditors on the cost of industry and debtors.

Britain suffered serious impacts of the reversal to the gold standard. The prices of the British goods increased. It faced the difficulty in the competition with the U.S., Germany and other industrialized nations in the trade. The English faced the growth of the unemployment. The strike in coal industry and the mutiny in the Atlantic sailors took place.

Britain was highly indebted to the U.S. Therefore, the English supremacy, exchange business, bankers' business, banking business and the seat of financial power and prestige were endangered. The U.S-British Struggle was manifested in the form of the disbursement of the long-term and the short-term loans also. The U.S. had abundant money and the capital to offer the long-term loans, on low interest rate and the countries like Canada, South Africa, Australia and other countries accepted the offer of the long-term loan.

The countries which took the long-term loans were mostly the British Colonies. To counter the U.S. policy, Britain offered the short-term loans to the banks of Central Europe. In competition of the long-term and the short-term loans the capital was poured into Europe. Consequently, millionaires cropped up in Europe and a new business of financing started.

The money was borrowed in New York at 2 percent and

was given to the banks, the bankers and the entrepreneurs at 6 percent in Berlin which went to Vienna at 8 percent. The British banks, taking the loan at 2 percent from France, gave to the German banks at 5-6 percent which was further given to Vienna at 8-9 percent and finally it reached Balkans (Hungary etc.) at the rate of 12 percent.

The whole of the European capitalist and the imperialist system was based on the cut-throat competition and the brutal rivalry. The U.S. was far ahead in the strength and resources than England. Bitterness between the two nations reached at height and there was only two options either struggle or the gradual transfer of the power.

England was interested in none. It was neither interested in giving up the imperial exploitation nor in the gradual transfer of the power to the U.S. The U.S. was interested in the both. The struggle for the supremacy too was one of the reasons behind the World War Second.

All the old sources of the power, the prestige and the strength were drying up but the English were not prepared to take back seat in the world affairs. In 1931, the financial system and the banks in Germany collapsed which led the crisis in England as it could not meet its liabilities and came on the verge to collapse. To save their capital, the British capitalists sent it abroad.

On September 23, 1931, England had to abandon the gold standard forever, in order to save her gold. In that situation one who had pound sterling could not exchange gold 'in lieu of' pound sterling, as could do before. The pound was forced away from the gold standard by the action of other countries. De-valuation of pound was a great event from the point of view of the British Empire and the English World. It was the beginning of the end of the British Empire. September 23, 1931, the day of the abandoning of the gold standard by England, is the date of historic event in the world history.

5

The Great Depression

After World War First, from 1919 to 1929, the U.S. was the only country that was prosperous overflowing with the capital. The finance is a sector of an economy which gives too much profit without producing anything and it was much developed in the U.S. economy. The Americans had capital and money in excess and they invested much more in the stock-market for the purchase of the securities, bonds and the shares.

The stock-market continued to rise because of the speculation. On the other hand, the U.S. was creditor to almost every nation in the World and it stopped the credit to Germany and some other countries. The result of which was the failure of some banks in Germany and stoppage of the repayment of the reparations and debts.

Many of the South American and other smaller Governments began to default because of the stoppage of the credit by the U.S. which was due to sudden collapse of the stock-market in the U.S. on 29th October, 1929, known as 'Black Tuesday'. It was a severe crisis in the financial circle of New York. From the day of the beginning of the crisis, October 29th, 1929, the U.S. lined up with other nations suffering from the crisis.

Initially it was a crisis of the trade and the industry beginning with crash in the stock-market and fall of banks in the U.S. By 1932 more than 5000 banks had failed, unemployment had reached 24.9 percent, businesses and families had defaulted on record number of loans. Tens of thousands of the Americans had become homeless.

In the beginning it was a problem of the American stock-market and small banks but later on it spread to the stock-markets and banks of European countries. South American nations failed because of the stoppage of the credit by the American banks and the money lenders. The major impacts of the crisis or the depression were:

1. Sharp fall in prices of agricultural products which affected adversely the agrarian community in the U.S. and other nations, as the U.S. was a big agricultural nation.
2. Problem of over-production in industrial sector, what so be the cause, it was apparently because of the reduced purchasing power of the masses.
3. Closure of the factories increased because of under selling of the products.
4. Unemployment increased because of closure of the factories.
5. International trade plunged by half to two third and so were the personal income, tax revenue, prices and profits.
6. Industry based cities were hard hit than the small cities.
7. Construction work stopped.
8. Primary activities like farming, mining and lumbering suffered the most as they were the suppliers of raw material for industries.

In India, the most serious sufferers were the rural people, farmers, peasants because of fall in the prices of agricultural products. The food was cheap but farmers and peasant who produced food starved. Even after selling all the agricultural produce they could not meet out their contingent and regular expenditures which made them foodless and penniless. They had to pay rent to the landlord and revenue to the Government in cash.

Similarly the debt of the urban poor increased because of the expenditures which were fixed in nature such as–taxes, rents, other utility services and the interest charges which were to be paid in cash. What was left after making such expenditures was not sufficient to support the life. Both, the rural and the urban poor felt the tragic brought by the crisis.

Among the industrialized nations, the U.S. was the last to be hit but reaction in the country and the people was sharp. The Americans were not accustomed to the hardship, crisis, unemployment, hunger and slow-starvation which led the cracking up of the national morale.

The confidence in banks and investment was shaken because of the failure of banks and sinking of stock-market. Money was withdrawn from the banks and was hoarded in the houses. Dwindling confidence and credit led the thousands banks down. The banks after banks sank but the big banks did not sink, which sank were the smaller ones.

Hunger and unemployment created a situation in which children were forced to work in the filthy sweet-shops, grown in smaller towns and cities. The children of 12 to 16 years were made to work for 10 to 12 hours a day for small wages. The children had to work in mills and factories also. To prohibit such abuses Labour Laws were enacted in the U.S. During the period there was deprivation and starvation, on a scale that the industrialized nations had never seen and experienced before.

Decline in the U.S. economy was set in later months of 1930 and reached at nadir by March 1933. The U.S. economy pulled most of the economies of the World down. After sinking of the most robust and dynamic economy of the U.S. none was left unaffected.

How people lived during the crisis is miserable story. They adapted moneyless system of livelihood. Barter system developed between the village and the urban dwellers. It was also made to use amongst the developed nations with their respective products.

One single cause was not responsible for such a crisis, the Great Depression, of the global extent which remained for a decade. There were many causes like the Germans believed that the real cause was the reparation and for other Europeans the war-debt. The monetary policy and shortage of gold were the causes for some others.

The economic nationalism, skewed distribution of the wealth, recession cycle, decline in the international trade, lower aggregate expenditure in the economy, massive decline in the income and so on were the real causes which surfaced up in the academic analysis.

The wealth and the capital accumulated in the Western Europe was the result of the exploitation of the colonies in previous centuries. The economy of the capitalist world grew by adding new markets, developing new industries and revitalizing the old industries in their countries in a cut-throat competition amongst industrialized nations.

The Wórld suffered the 'long depression' from 1873 to 1896 which was overcome by developing and exploiting new areas which were left so far by the colonizers through the incorporation of the new consumers and markets in the world economy. It is evident by the expansion of the Colonial Empires during 1890-1900.

During the 20th century, with the arrival of Germany, the U.S., France and other countries of the Western Europe in the core of the world economy it became multi-nodal which was the British dominated earlier. The nations of the core economy started partial protectionism and developed the concept of 'the economic nationalism', emphasizing on 'buy home-made goods' which spread in the peripheral nations as well.

Awakening in the East took place in the early 20th century which aroused the down-trodden people in countries like India. The Indians aligned behind Mahatma Gandhi who infused sense of pride in the half naked people as Gandhiji himself was leading the life in a manner of 'half naked Faquir or Saint'.

Gandhiji's 'charkha' or spinning wheel was a symbol of the home industry. He emphasized on the reducing demand and depending on 'home-made goods', the theme behind the economic nationalism.

The message of Gandhiji spread like fire in the bush throughout India and its flares were felt elsewhere as well. India is a vast country with large population and is a big market. Hundred years ago England was in a position to get consumed its fifty percent of the cotton-good-exports in India that was not possible in 1920s.

Thus, because of the awakening in the East, economic nationalism and revival of industries in the colonies like India, the colonial markets shrank for the colonial powers like England etc.

A huge market of USSR was out of the capitalist economy because of the October Revolution and establishment of the Communism which further reduced the market for industrialized nations. USSR was supplying the agricultural produce to the nations of Europe.

Much more borrowing took place during World War First and aftermath. Almost all the nations of Europe were indebted especially to the U.S. The debts were of the three kinds:

1. Reparations–defeated countries were forced to pay war-indemnity to the victorious nations.
2. Inter-Governmental debt- Allied countries owed to each other and especially to the U.S.
3. National debt–each country had borrowed from its own citizens.

Germany wiped off all the national debt by means of inflation. To some extent France reduced its national debt in the similar way.

Bonds were issued to borrow from the people of a country. People who had surplus money bought the bonds so the bond holders were the rich. Government levied tax on all the citizens, the poor and the rich. After taxation the Government accumulated some wealth and bought back the bonds from the people. In this way the national loans were returned to the people.

Thus, the rich paid taxes and got their lent money back from the Government, in the form of selling of bonds to the Government. The rich became richer whereas the poor became poorer as they paid taxes and got nothing. The purchasing power of the poor got reduced.

The rich over-invested in the fresh factories, the machinery and other capital expenditures. They invested in the capital and the stock-markets and aired the speculation. They produced goods on mass scale and the poor buyers had no money to buy. Thus, the problem of the over-production and the under-selling arose. In this way, industries got set-back and the problem of the unemployment deepened.

The money which could have been in hands of public to buy goods was concentrated in a few rich hands who did not know what was to be done with it. The excess money from the U.S. flowed to the nations of South America, Eastern Europe and Germany. The borrowings from the U.S. kept on the war-torn Europe alive for sometime. The stoppage of the lending brought the crash in the economies finally.

The democrats believed that the problem arose because of too much money in hands of the business class and similarly the U.S. President F.D. Roosevelt blamed the big business for creating unstable bubble in the economy. For him, New Deal was the remedy which empowered labour unions and farmers and raised taxes on corporate profits.

John Maynard Keynes, the famous economist, argued that the decline in the income and the employment well below the average was because of the low aggregate expenditure made in the economy.

Marriner S. Eccles was Chairman of Federal Reserve of the U.S. from November 1934 to February '48. He has depicted the causes of the 'Great Depression' in his memoir, 'Beckoning Frontiers' (New York, Alfred A. Knopf, 1951).

"As mass production has to be accompanied by mass consumption, in turn implies a distribution of wealth, not of existing wealth, but of wealth as it is currently produced, to provide men with buying power equal to amount of goods and services offered by nation's economic machinery."

He further adds "...had there been less savings by business and higher income groups and more income in the lower groups, we should have had far greater stability in our economy. Had the six billion dollars, for instance, that were loaned by corporations and wealthy individuals for stock-market speculation been distributed to the public as lower prices or higher wages with less profits to the corporations and the well-to-do, it would have prevented or greatly moderated the economic collapse that began at the end of 1929."

Britain was the first to recover from the 'depression' with the help of the Empire. The hidden resources and gold of the British Empire particularly of India and Egypt were utilized in the British interest. The de-linking of the British pound from the gold standard helped in the increase of the British exports as they had become cheaper in the foreign markets. The impact of the de-linking of pound from gold standard varied widely.

Recovery in the U.S. began in 1933 with programmes of the New Deal, introduced by President F.D. Roosevelt but when the programmes were lifted in 1937, the crisis came back. Finally, the World War Second took the crisis away. Recovery in the U.S. is credited partly to the gold inflow, partly to the de-valuation of dollar and partly to the deteriorating political situations in Europe.

The relatively high level self-sufficient France suffered less in the crisis. USSR was not totally unaffected because it exported the agricultural products to Europe and got less return. In general the 'depression' lasted for ten years up to 1939, when World War Second broke out.

One of the significant effects of the 'Great Depression' was the liberation of the British colonies of European origin like-Canada, Australia, New Zealand, South Africa etc. In Mid-1930s Japan and Italy expanded colonial possessions. The U.S. replaced classical economic liberal approach by the Keynesian one. Keynes became the guiding economist for second half of the twentieth century.

6

Mid of the Twentieth Century

After September 23, 1931, when England departed from the gold standard, it was no longer the supreme power in the World despite its large Colonial Empire. Now the superiority of the U.S. was established.

The emergence of the U.S. as the supreme power and beginning of planned economic development in USSR were the simultaneous events. With such a development the World got divided into the two blocs, i.e., capitalist and communist blocs. The capitalist world was led by the U.S. and the communist world was led by USSR and such a division led to the beginning of the cold war between the two.

Prof. Nicholas J. Spykman, an American geo-political thinker, drew attention to overseas empire and the maritime mobility as a basis of a new type of geo-political structure in contrast to the former pattern of the great land powers. He emphasized that "it is sea power which has made it possible to conceive of the Eurasian continent as a unit and it is sea power which governs the relationship between the Old and the New Worlds".

Spykman's prescription became the basis, at least in part, of the American policy of "containment"-the policy of surrounding and sealing the Heartland fortress i.e. the Communist bloc. Asia, Africa and a part of Europe, the region surrounding USSR, along with the overseas empire were the focus of the American geo-political thinkers.

Spykman prescribed that Allied powers should base their policies on preventing any consolidation of USSR and communists in Asia, Africa and a part of Europe, i.e., in the rimland. Fall of any country of the rimland to USSR would frustrate the economic and political interests of the U.S.

Keeping in mind the geo-political situation, Spykman emphasized on the following maxim for the global power politics – "Who controls the rimland rules Eurasia;

Who rules Eurasia controls the destinies of the World."

Throughout the Cold-War period the geo-political theory of Spykman played a crucial role in the American policy and the global politics. The theory lost its significance with the demise of USSR in 1991.

By 1940s, the American economy had become so strong that it needed large market which was only in rimland and that was in hands of the European Colonial Powers. The same markets of the third world were required for the U.S. supremacy and economic development in the second half of the twentieth century. USSR was economically and politically interested in the direct access to the harbours of the Indian Ocean via nations of the rimland.

The prime objectives of the U.S. were to prevent the nations of rimland from going in the bloc of USSR and to increase the market under the canopy of free trade and free nation. To increase the sphere of influence was the need of the hour for the U.S. To ensure it, expansion of the Communism was to be contained. At the same time nations of rimland were to be protected from the military aggressions of USSR and they were to be made free from the colonial yoke also.

The sphere of influence of the U.S. was North and South Americas as well as Caribbean Islands by the early years of the twentieth century. To increase it, de-colonization of the nations of the rimland was essential. The British hold over the most part of rimland was the main hurdle in the path of the U.S. ambition. Therefore, the U.S. followed the policy of de-colonization and pressurized England to dismantle the British Empire as soon as possible.

The colonialism and the imperialism have been the profit-oriented enterprises since the beginning. It served the economic as well as the political interests of the colonial powers for long time. The colonies were the source of the bread and butter of colonizers but all the colonies were not equally profitable at a point of time.

Some colonies were not left profitable after the exploitation of hundreds of years. After exhaustion of mineral resources, the mineral rich colonies were no longer profitable. When cheaper raw materials were found elsewhere, the previous colonies proved unfruitful. In the colonies where cost of combating freedom struggle increased, the colonies became liabilities instead of the assets for the 'mother 'country.

Therefore, the freedom on such colonies was thrust upon when they became unprofitable like Canada, Australia, New Zealand, West Indies, Afghanistan, Persia and so on after the World War First.

In the early 20th century, the concept of the welfare of the people of the colonies arose and was considered in administrative policies. In many cases "burden of the Empire had begun to outweigh the advantage of the Empire". In that situation, many people in England, France and other imperial countries echoed the words of Rudyard Kipling, "take up white man's burden."

But significance of colonies continued in 20th century as well. It was evident by the German, the Italian and the Japanese expansion of colonies in 1930s. The colonial powers of Europe crippled by the Second World War were no longer able to contain the rising tide of the nationalism for independence in the colonies. In mid-20th century, the old repressive policies could not be followed in the enlightened atmosphere of the World.

The end of the old colonial system was, therefore, imperative in the effective influence of the U.S., the leading power of the day. Wise Imperialists like Britain agreed to transfer the power smoothly and peacefully. In the colonies which were under control of the lesser wise people the transfer of the power was through armed conflict.

Thus, de-colonization began in 1940s and by mid-1960s most of the nations got freedom. The newly liberated countries of third world are highly grateful and thankful to the U.S. and England who started the process of the de-colonization.

F.D. Roosevelt, the U.S. President had outlined the plan for the world economic order, to come in effect after the Second World War. But the old colonial structure did not end abruptly rather it continued with its conspicuous feature of 'core-periphery' model of the world economy. After the War, only economy which was strong, diversified and sustainable was that of the U.S., the dominant economy in the World.

Other economies of Europe and Japan were torn by the War badly. In the new world order too, the economies of the peripheral nations were made subordinate to the economic needs of the core countries dominated by the U.S. which enjoyed the supply of the required resources from all parts of the World and made use of the markets which were hitherto not available to the U.S. In due course of time, under the pressure of external forces, the core-periphery relationship weakened.

Up to the mid-1960s, the industrialization was continued in the U.S. The industries grew in number and size with employment generation. In 1960s, the factory managers and owners began shutting down their factories in the U.S. and moved them to Mexico, China, South Korea, Taiwan, India and a number of the third world nations. Consequently, the U.S. got reduced to a nation of the service jobs. The main industries which were left in the U.S. were the aeroplane industry and the agriculture.

The de-industrialization of the U.S. was begun when the productivity was declining and the trade deficit was rising. The global economic system entered in the crisis in mid-1960s when the economic development was approaching towards stagnation at the given level of the technological innovations.

Until 1965, the third world nations were implementing the development plans based on their national priority. In India, up to the Third Five Year Plan, the national priorities got reflected in the development plans and programmes.

The IMF devised structural adjustment programmes came into the operation after 1965. Pressures of the IMF and other agencies were mounting on the economies of the third world for changing the priorities covertly in favour of the U.S. and other industrialized nations.

Thereafter, under the Western pressure the nation-oriented plans in the third world were abandoned. The attempts were made to transform the economies of the third world export-oriented. The export-oriented growth is a feature of the colonial economy. After de-colonization it should have been abandoned but ironically it was established and strengthened in the name of the development.

Whole of the World can't be benefited by the single model, i.e., export-oriented model. The industrialized world was exporting manufactured goods but developing world did not have anything to export except the raw materials and the agricultural products which they had been exporting since the colonial period.

Thus, the export-oriented growth model brought the third world in the colonial economic relations back. The third world was still denied of the industrial development and was being kept in the old fashion of economic relation in the name of the development.

Europe and Japan had recovered from the effects of Second World War by 1960s and were ready to supply the consumer goods to the rest of the World. Now there were three groups of the suppliers of industrial products, the U.S., Europe and Japan. The buyers were the newly liberated nations of Asia and Africa along with the weaker South American nations.

Nobody was thinking about the purchasing power of the masses which is the bedrock of the economic development. Perhaps the world did not want to bring the third world out of the colonial hangover. At the same time the Western World wanted to sell their products in the markets of the East where there was a little purchasing power at all.

BrettonWoods System

Precursor of the Bretton Woods system was Atlantic Charter drafted during the meeting of the U.S. President F.D. Roosevelt with the British Prime Minister Winston Churchill in August, 1941 on a ship in the North Atlantic Ocean. The Atlantic charter affirmed the right to all nations regarding access to the trade and the raw materials. The Charter affirmed freedom of sea, disarmament of aggressors and establishment of a wide and permanent system of general security. Bretton Woods Agreement was the greatest blow to Britain next to the World War Second.

The post-war world economic system was conceptualized during the War. Bretton Woods Agreement, signed during July, 1944 by the 44 allied nations, gave the rules regarding the commercial and the financial relations and the monetary management in the mid-20th century. To regulate the international monetary system the rules, the institutions and the procedures were set-up. At BrettonWoods, the International Monetary Fund and the International Bank for Reconstruction and Development were established.

Unlike a national economy, the international economy lacks the Central Bank and the Central Government that can issue a currency and manage its use. A system of pegged rate of currencies, managed by a series of newly created international institutions, using the U.S. dollar as a reserve currency which was the gold standard, was set-up. Thus, in the place of the former fixed-rate-currency-system, the pegged-rate-currency-system came into the being.

The member nations of the new currency system were required to establish a parity of their national currencies in terms of gold (a peg) and to maintain exchange rates with plus minus one percent, of the peg (gold). It was obligatory to each nation to adopt such a monetary policy. The U.S. dollar took over the role which was played by gold under the gold standard financial system. In face of the increasing strain, the system collapsed in 1971.

International Monetary Fund provides loan to the member countries in the event of the current account deficit or the balance of payment crisis or any other contingency. The quantum of borrowing depends on the size of the economy represented in the form of quota which is larger for the larger economies and smaller far the smaller ones. Thus, the IMF was and is under the control of the big economies which have more roles to play.

In practice, the IMF has been instrumental in implementing the policies of the U.S. The IMF protected the stronger economies from the disruption of the international trade and the growth. The voting rights depend on the quota or the contributions made to the IMF. The U.S. has one third of the quota which is enough to veto all the changes to the IMF charter.

International Bank for Reconstruction and Development was set-up to promote the growth of the world trade and to finance the post-war re-construction of Europe. It is a specialized agency to make loans for the economic development purposes.

Another institution, International Development Agency, was created in 1961 to expand the global economy.

The International Bank for Reconstruction and Development and the International Development Agency form the World Bank.

The World Bank Group consists of the following five institutions:

1. IBRD-International Bank for Reconstruction and Development.
2. IDA-International Development Agency.
3. IFC-International Finance Corporation.
4. MIGA-Multilateral Investment Guarantee Agency.
5. ICSID-International Centre for Settlement of Investment Dispute.

After Second World War, the U.S. took control over the monetary policy of the World through BrettonWoods

Institutions, the IMF and the IBRD. The capitalist world was suffering from the huge dollar shortage as the U.S. had surplus balance of trade and the dollar was not going out of the U.S., so the rest of the World was lacking the dollar.

By 1947, IMF and IBRD both were admitting that they could not deal with the problems of international monetary system. To increase the liquidity in the international market the grants-in-aid programmes were set-up by the U.S. in 1950s so that dollar could out flow from the U.S. in the rest of the World.

The European Recovery Programmes were set-up to run through the grants-in-aid from the U.S. instead of the loans from IMF because the IMF loans proved insufficient to bring back the war-torn European economy on the track and to correct their balance of payment deficit.

During 1947-58, the U.S. encouraged out flow of the dollars. The U.S. grants-in-aid for Europe and Japan went for re-building the productivity and the export capacity. It was anticipated that the stronger economy of Europe and that of Japan would benefit the U.S. by increasing the market and creating the new space for the capital investment.

The global economy was expanding in the second half of the 20th century. Some institutions were created and put in the World Bank Group to boost the global growth like the International Finance Corporation created in 1956 and the International Development Agency created in 1961.

The International Development Agency has been instrumental in pressurizing the developing economies to open their markets. It provided agricultural loans for the Green Revolution in 1960s. It stabilized and occasionally subsidized the Governments in Latin America in particular and those in the third world in general.

During the colonial period Asia and Africa were out of the American sphere of influence. In the post-colonial era whole of the World came under the American influence and the U.S. was the only strong and robust economy doing trade all over the World.

The U.S., using the new financial and monetary policy and convertible financial system, earned the tremendous profits from the third world trade as the second world, under leadership of USSR was closed in itself and it was the U.S. which was alone strong economy in the first world.

The post-colonial era was the period when the American industries and the trade expanded harnessing market and the raw materials and other resources over the globe. It was the period of the development and social change in the American society for instance the proportion of women in services started increasing during 1960s.

The U.S. used the profits, earned from the trade with the third world, in providing grants-in-aid to the European nations and Japan to re-build their economies. The trade surplus made it easier to the U.S. to invest outside especially in Europe. The dollar continued to remain the indicator of the strength of the world economy.

The BrettonWoods financial system collapsed when the U.S. trade with the third world was destabilized after the economic re-emergence of Europe and Japan, in early 1970s.

In a response to the recession in the U.S. economy in 1958, Eisenhower Administration placed the import quota on the oil, inter-alia other restrictions placed on the trade outflow. The restrictions were insufficient to counter the recession.

There was a need to make changes in the monetary policy, in the wake of the recession, to make the system workable. Either alteration of peg of dollar to gold or to maintain the free market price of the gold closer to $35/ounce was needed. The high market price of the gold was temptating the buying of the gold at BrettonWoods price and selling it in the free market.

To increase the production capacity and to encourage exports, Kennedy administration drafted the tax-cut programme in the tax-system with the radical changes focusing on maintaining the gold price at US$ 35/ounce. It was an attempt made to adhere to the peg of the dollar.

In this regard, the perspective of the U.S. President Lyndon Baines Johnson is as follows:

"World supply of gold is insufficient to make the present system workable, particularly the use of dollar as a reserve currency is essential to create the required liquidity to sustain world trade and growth."

The decline of the International Monetary Management was surfaced with the structural changes of 1960s which made currencies convertible again. The currencies of the nations of the Western Europe had become convertible at the end of 1958 and Japanese Yen in 1964. The convertibility facilitated the expansion of the international financial transaction which deepened the monetary inter-dependence.

The growth of the International Currency Market was another structural change of 1960s and various banks formed International syndicates in 1964. By 1971, over three fourth of the World's largest banks had become share-holders in such syndicates.

Multi-national banks can and do make huge international transfer of the capital for the investment purposes including investment in the derivatives like hedging and speculating against exchange rate fluctuations. The new form of the monetary inter-dependence made possible huge capital flow across the nations.

By mid-1960s the European Economic Community and Japan had become again the international economic powers on their own right. Their total foreign exchange reserves exceeded that of the U.S. with higher trade and economic growth and per capita income approaching to that of the U.S., Europe and Japan were narrowing gaps between themselves and with the U.S. also.

The global core economy was becoming multi-nodal with three main centres of the economic power, namely the U.S., the European Economic Community and Japan. The privileged role of the dollar as an international currency became endangered. The dollar was the foundation that had underpinned the post-1945 global trading system.

In effect, the U.S. with its deposits determined the level of the international liquidity. In an increasingly inter-dependent world the U.S. policy greatly influenced the economies of Europe and Japan.

At the time of the creation of the Bretton Woods system, the U.S. was producing half of the World's manufactured goods and had half of the World's foreign exchange reserve.

After the World War Second the U.S. had two burdens, the international management and the cold war. Throughout 1950s the U.S. sustained deficit balance of payment in order to finance loans, grants-in-aid and troops for allied regime. During 1960s, the cost of the U.S. burden became less bearable and remained within the tolerance limit.

In 1967, the IMF agreed to replace the tranche division, set-up in 1946, by the Special Drawing Rights at Rio-de-Janeiro, a city of Brazil. The Special Drawing Right was set equal to the one dollar. The SDRs could be used between the banks and IMF and for other transactions they could not be used as its liquidity was less.

Hence, the use of SDR was restricted; each nation could hold SDR three times of the allotment quota by paying the interest. The original interest rate was 1.5 percent. The interest payment was a preventive measure. It aimed to restrict nations from buying pegged gold and selling it at higher rate in the free market.

The reasons were to be given to hold dollars by crediting interest more than the limit as there was a clear limit to the quantum of dollar which could be held by a nation. For SDR, market could not be created but the value of relationship was monetized. It seems that SDR system has offered a way to balance the system. The SDR, used as the paper gold, seemed to change the World's banker. Earlier the U.S. was the World's banker but now IMF became that of the World.

On March 17, 1968, London Gold Pool, created on November1, 1961 was dissolved as there was run on the gold and outflow of gold from the U.S. was accelerated. Various attempts were made to defend the dollar at the fixed peg of US$ 35/ounce in the U.S. The policies of Eisenhower, Kennedy and Johnson administrations became increasingly untenable regarding the defence of the dollar at fixed peg.

As a final attempt to defend the dollar the control over the foreign investment including mandatory investment and that on the currency were tightened in 1968. A series of meetings began to rescue or reform the existing system. In November 1968 attempts to maintain the peg of dollar collapsed.

A new policy was attempted to convert the Bretton Woods system where the enforcement mechanism floated by some means would be set by either fiat or by a restriction to honour the foreign accounts. The International Monetary Management got paralyzed with the induction of the floating Bretton Woods System, during 1968-'72.

By 1970s the U.S. had just fewer than 16 percent of the international foreign exchange reserves. In the changing atmosphere and the ground realities the U.S. commitment and burden transformed into the impediments in the path of the fixed exchange rate and the U.S. obligation to convert the dollar into the gold on a demand. The U.S. President Nixon de-linked the dollar from the peg of gold, making dollar inconvertible to the gold directly except in the open market, in 1971.

The structural changes of 1970s accelerated the decline of the U.S. monetary influence in the World which undermined the international monetary management. As a result of the changes which took place within the nation and elsewhere the U.S. was no longer as strong (or alone) economic power as was for last more than two decades.

After 1971, the gold became floating assets and the exchange rate reached at US$ 44.2/ounce. The exchange rate got increased up to the US$ 70.3/ounce in 1972. The devaluation of the dollar was done by the Smithsonian Agreement which was created by a meeting of 'Group of Ten' in Smithsonian Institute of Washington. The Smithsonian Agreement failed to impose the discipline on the U.S. Government with no other credibility mechanism in place.

By 1972, currencies began abandoning even the de-valued peg against the dollar. It took a decade for all the industrialized nations to do so. In February 1973 BrettonWoods currency market of exchange closed after de-valuation of the dollar to the US$ 44/ounce and re-opened in March that year in the floating currency regime.

By 1976, all the major currencies were floating. Exchange rates were no longer principle of the monetary policy.

BrettonWoods System II is a system of the currency relations evolved after 2001. In it the currencies, particularly Chinese renminbi (yuan), remained fixed to the U.S. dollar. The argument is that a system of pegged currencies is both stable and desirable.

In October, 2008, Argentine President Cristina Fernandez de Kirchner said, "the financial world crises will need a strong regulation in the matters of financial markets and capital movement throughout the World. A new Bretton Woods will be needed."

7

Multinational Corporations and Liberalization

The multinational corporation is a manifestation of the inter-dependency relations amongst the nations of the World. There are several other mechanisms which also maintain the dependency relation between the nations in the World like-international trade, international labour migration, foreign-aid, technology transfer etc.

The capitalist world had acquired qualitatively new characteristics by 1965. The production system was broken up into the horizontal and the vertical segments and had spread world-wide through multinational corporations. The capitalist production system is a complex web of diverse strands like the multinational corporations, international trade, foreign-aid, technology transfer and so on.

The multinational corporations operate in a very different manner but whatever may be they are the modern version of the mercantilist trade of the era of the Economic Revolution. They are registered companies and firms in a country and work in many countries and command vast amount of resources in the form of capital, technology, managerial expertise and information. Many of them are involved in product innovation, research and development. They make direct foreign investments across the countries and trade with goods and services.

Operations of the multinational corporations are separated in such a way that they take advantage of the inexpensive raw materials, cheap labour force and the large markets of the third world. They operate in various parts of the World depending on the product and its market. They maintain a global operating network and their profit margin increases through the overseas investment.

One group of the scholars suggests that multinational corporations make direct investment in the poor countries, transfer advanced technologies, create jobs and help them in harnessing natural resources. But it is not so, as the projected beneficial results of their economic activities appear shallow when examined critically. A few of them are involved in such an activity which creates more jobs for the people.

Most of the multinational corporations are involved in the maximization of their profit margins. In general, it is not producing long-term benefits for the general people or economies of the host country.

The multinational corporations transfer firm-specific technology which has a little general application and hamper economic growth in the host country in general. Because of the excess flooding of products of the multinational corporations the demand and the sale of the domestic products get reduced in the developing world where they operate.

Thus, the multinational corporations inhibit the expansion of the local industries thereby reduces the employment opportunities in the poor nations where they operate. The losses occurred by them could be overcome by expanding new activities and investing in the field of the high-technology for the traditional industries. But it would reduce their profit margins, for which they seem not to be prepared.

The vulnerable third world economies became victim of the foreign investment in the form of external debt, dependency on technology and an enslaved consumption pattern. Their further development comes under the subject to the redeployment of the trans-national capital. It erodes the autonomy of the third world nations regarding their national plans and policies. It reduces the ruling class of these nations to a set of "sub-ordinate and powerless transition-belt for the world capital."

In the interest of the multinational corporations the U.S. has been interfering in the national plans and programmes in the third world. In 1958, during the foreign exchange crisis, India was arm-twisted by the U.S. and was compelled to modify its industrial policy by relaxing terms and conditions for the foreign collaborations. Whenever India was in the problems like foreign exchange, loan or food grain crises, the U.S. arm-twisted and compelled to compromise with the national priorities in the favour of multinational corporations.

When the global economic system plunged into the crisis in the mid-1960s, the already weaker Indian economy could not withstand the adverse external pressure. It abandoned whatever was left of its earlier semi-autonomous model of the development. In 1966, the World Bank directed to re-order the investment priorities indicating that India's autonomy was forfeited with respect to the major economic policies and plans in the favour of the multinational corporations, the instrument of the global hegemony of the West.

Liberalization refers to the relaxation of the restrictions, in the field of the socio-economic policies, of the previous Governments. In the U.S. social relaxation started with the entry of women in the non-agrarian work-force and other progressive reforms made in the society in 1960s. The economic liberalization of the U.S. was related to the relaxation in the rules and regulations regarding the trade and the capital markets associated with the privatization of the public sector enterprises, in 1960s.

The de-industrialization of the U.S. began with emphasis on the multinational corporations, free trade and open market when the economic growth was slowing down in 1960s. The economic growth was stagnant and the inflation was rising in 1970s. The focus of the U.S. Government was to control the inflation for which the measures of 'wage and price control' were introduced under the President Nixon.

1970s was the worst decade for economies of the West. The U.S. economic performance was the worst since the Great Depression of 1929. The growth rate was reduced in comparison to the previous decades of high standing enjoyed by the U.S. economy. The high domestic spending begun during the Kennedy administration gradually became unglued.

The events of early 1970s led to the de-regulation of the economy. In 1971, the dollar was de-linked from the gold standard which was the basis of the U.S. monetary policy. In 1973, the OPEC members worked out to control the oil prices at uniform level and raised the prices of crude oil from US$ 2.95 per barrel in later months of 1973 to US$ 11.65 per barrel in early 1974. The concept of demand and supply and no alternative to the petroleum in short run compelled the buyer nations to succumb to the pressure of the OPEC.

The rise in the petroleum prices caused balance of payment crises in so many countries. The oil producing and exporting countries became virtual regulator of the world economy. The rise in the oil prices caused an increase in the inflation throughout the World. The oil crisis prevented the third world from getting benefits of the Green Revolution of 1960s and withheld their development, keeping them in the poverty. At the same time in 1970s Europe got recovered from the war hang-over with the help of the grants-in-aid programmes under the Marshal Plan of 1950s.

The era of economic de-regulation lasted from 1974 to 1992, during which the New Deal Regulations, started by President Roosevelt after the 'Great Depression' of 1929 and some other regulations regarding loans and savings were removed. The Keynesian economic theory was replaced by Neo-liberal economic theory under Margaret Thatcher, then British Prime Minister.

The economic performance of the West and certainly of the U.S. was not as good as happened to be earlier. The growth was lower and inflation was higher throughout much of the World. Manufacturing industries in the U.S. had begun to decline with last trade surplus in 1975 whereas the Japanese economy was continuing to expand.

It was the time of the beginning of the IMF devised policies of the structural adjustment programmes which were meant to re-structure the economies of the World and were based on "one size fits all" prescription which did not help much of the population in the World. The third world had to suffer its disastrous consequences. Because the different nations have the different problems with their specific solutions which could not be solved by the prescription "one size fits all."

The rich countries don't need the Bretton Woods Institutions. These institutions are a need of the poor nations which don't have any say in them. Almost all the nations of the World were made to pursue the same policy of making structural adjustment in consonance with the policies of the globalization sponsored by the IMF, under neo-liberal economic theory.

In 1970s, 'export, import led growth strategies' were adopted world-over in the various political regimes, for instance:

- Communist Party led Governments in Poland, Rumania and Hungary of Eastern Europe.
- Military dictatorship Governments in Argentina, Brazil, Chile and Pakistan.
- Democratic Governments of Lebanon and Indonesia.

In 1980s, the same 'IMF imposed structural adjustment policies' were implemented and adopted by all types of Governments with different intensities of pursuance. The countries, not even under the IMF and World Bank purview, followed the IMF-Style structural adjustment policies, like Poland which was not the member of IMF and Nicaragua which had no access to the IMF credit.

During 1970s and 1980s, IMF was instrumental in the globalization of the economies in the World with its strategies and policies based on "one size fits all'' prescription.

Ironically, the economic changes could not give positive results in all type of Governments. It was a path of the growth of the economy based on import and external debt. The result of it was the growth in number of the high-capital-intensive industries contrary to the domestic-endowment-based ones.

The outcome of such a development was the concentration of the wealth in a few hands. Such a path of the development was the internally unsustainable and the externally vulnerable to the any adverse change in the external environment.

The structural changes compelled the nations of the third world to change their policies. Some of the changes were as follows:

1. States withdrew their hands from the economic activities.
2. The public enterprises and institutions of public welfare were privatized.
3. States reduced their expenditure on education, health and public services.
4. The concept of the 'public welfare-state' was discarded.
5. The state was no longer a shield to their people from the alien competition and the immigration.
6. States became fountain heads of corruption, nepotism and coercion.
7. The military and or the bureaucracy became the key institutions while the people oriented institutions weakened in many cases.
8. The erosion of the people oriented institutions led to the shrinking of the political space for the genuine opposition.
9. Reagonomics triggered a growth of the modern armament industry which heralded a new phase of the world capitalism.
10. Thatcher's public enterprises widened the economic power of the global capitalists.
11. The expansion of the multinational corporations and the international financial institutions integrated the national markets into the global market and the national elite into the global investors.
12. The 'Development Consensus' of 1960s was abandoned.
13. The national Governments lost the human-face and imbibed a new face of the multinational corporations.

Before the globalization and after World War Second, the

World was passing through the process of economic development. The process of the globalization had in fact de-legitimatized the whole process and paradigm of the development and provided an alternative model to the society and created an ideological vacuum.

The policies and the practices of 1980s focused on the supply side of economics and accentuated the consumerism in the society. It projected a new face of the capitalism which was a profit oriented and anti-welfare.

1960 onwards, many nations attempted liberalization of their economies, relaxing them from previous restrictions and opening them for the wider world. But most of them did not get success and had to reverse the process of the liberalization.

The Brazilian, the Portuguese and the Spanish liberalization of 1960s were reversed after the first oil shock of 1973, when the oil price rise had created the balance of payment crisis. Peruvian liberalization which was begun in 1979 was aborted during early 1980s. Reforms of New Zealand (1979 and 1984) were gradual and unsuccessful. Zambian liberalization of 1985 began with a big bang without pre-announcement but collapsed within two years.

The twice born Kenyan liberalization (1981 and 1990) did not produce any notable success too. The Indian liberalization of 1991, born out of the panic and the external pressure, lost steam by 1993 too.

The fast track internally driven Chinese liberalization was begun in 1992 but the politically embarrassing economic dualism emerged. Consequently, the regulatory mechanism had to be reactivated in 1993.

Many countries of Latin America, Africa and Asia outside the city States of Hong-Kong and Singapore failed miserably in their pursuit of the IMF-style 'export, import led growth strategy.'

8

Later Years of the Twentieth Century

In the later years of the twentieth century centres of economic development went beyond the core area of the world economy. The newly industrialized nations emerged in East-Asia. Earlier Japan was the only industrialized nation in Asia. The period is conspicuous by absence of peace and tranquility in the sphere of global economy.

In the East-Asian nations of Hong Kong, Taiwan, South Korea and Singapore the rapid industrialization and the economic transformation took place in the wake of the export-driven-economic development combined with the educational and other policy reforms introduced by their Governments, in the phase of the liberalization and globalization.

The supporters of the globalization believe that industrialization in the region was due to the free market, open trade ideology and the IMF sponsored structural adjustment strategies of export-led-growth model. But it was not so, as the State intervention along with some other measures had been more important in the industrialization of the region.

Governments in these nations implemented the U.S. imposed land-reforms, utilized the massive cold war subsidies, protected and subsidized the industries. The nations of East-Asia attained their industrial development and the growth through the strategic planning.

In South Korea, there was an Economic Planning Board to undertake and guide the industrial development. Six industries-steel, metal, machine building, ship-building, electronics and chemicals were under the intense Government support. Despite stiff opposition from the IMF and the World Bank, heavy chemical industries were given the top priority.

The second tier of the newly industrialized countries of Asia included Thailand, Malaysia, Indonesia and other South-East Asian nations. During mid-1980s, Thai-Government overtly protected and encouraged the 'import-substituting' industries, giving impetus to the industrial development in the country.

In Malaysia, the development took place through industrial planning. In 1982, the Malaysian Government hooked up the automobile industry with Mitsubishi but ensured 80 percent local contents. Malaysia protected indigenous market and economic system integrating itself with the world market.

In Indonesia too, the industrial development was through the help of the national Government where the national aircraft industry was very important and was developed through the support of the State. 'Asian Tigers' developed industrially with the help of the State and openness of the economy both.

The industrial development in the East-Asian countries brought together income in-equality which created cleavages in the society and intensified the class conflict. It undermined agriculture and related activities and the benefits of 'Green Revolution' as well as degraded the environment.

The land-reforms which were introduced in South Korea and Taiwan in American influence during 1950s were reversed during 1970s when agricultural land were squeezed to build up industries, under the policy of export-led industrialization in East and South-East Asia.

Development is supposed to bring self-reliance in a nation but industrial development did not bring self-reliance, for instance in South Korea and Taiwan as they continued to remain crucially dependent on Japan in regard to the industrialization. For instance, in South Korea, 90 percent of machines were imported from Japan.

The economies of 'Asian Tigers' remained susceptible to the external economic forces as the profits from industries were invested in the real estate and the stock-markets for the short-term gains instead of strengthening the manufacturing, the trade and other economic activities.

The profits of the industrialization did not strengthen the national economy as they were not invested in real economy rather they were invested in financial economy which gave much profit to the investors without producing anything in the real economy. The trend continued till date and brought the problem in the economies of the different nations.

In plural societies like Indonesia and Malaysia, the industrialization brought the class-conflict creating cleavages in the social formations on the basis of the economic and the industrial development which accentuated economic inequality. The industrialization in these countries did not make the society egalitarian. The industrialization in Thailand brought deforestation, water pollution and ecological degradation causing hazardous consequences to the citizens.

In these societies democratic values were reduced as a consequence of the industrialization. Democratic assertion of the people was repressed by the State in favour of industrialization which neither increased job opportunity for the people nor encompassed masses in the process of industrialization. The people when asserted for the benefits of the masses, they were repressed. The foreign advisors in these nations asserted "growth first democracy later."

The instruments of the globalization were the 'free trade' and the 'open market' with the liberalization of the finance sector rules and the regulation for the capital flow, investment, banking, insurance and so on.

The most significant tendencies of globalization have been the monopoly and the speculation. The free and open markets always tended to monopoly, unless subjected to the civil regulations, asset-distribution and persist State-intervention. There was nothing inherently efficient in the free and open market. They didn't themselves promote the sound investment or the wise management.

When the assets, the wealth and the leverage become concentrated in a few hands then open market encourages nothing but gambling, masking itself as the sound investment as happens, for instance, in the derivative markets.

Another tendency encouraged by the free and open market is speculation, the driving force of capital market in financial economy. The speculative and the monopolistic global capitalists operate on larger scale. They make deals in hundreds of countries as well as in a variety of cultures.

The capitalists are little concerned to the people and economies of the nations where they work. They are interested in the maximization of their profit, for which they need a handful of people who have purchasing power for their products.

The global capitalists and the owners of the multi-national corporations did not try to expand the number of people involved in the multi-national business. It was not their duty to do so. To increase the purchasing power, consequently, to generate demand for industrially-produced goods and services is the duty of the national Governments in particular and of the U.N. in general which performs the role of the global government.

The U.N., the world body to look-after the affairs of the World, hardly went beyond the interests of the multi-national corporations and the industrial world as it is severely gripped in the hands of the U.S. and other industrialized western nations whose role is dubious. They seem the custodian of the interests of the multi-national corporations not of the global people in general.

The size of the global economy got increased but the number of participants, involved in the economic affairs, in proportion to the whole of the population of the World, did not increase much, due to the monopoly exercised by the multi-national corporations.

The poverty in the World increased which is evident from the reduced purchasing power of the masses but the production and the productivity gone up. What is more significant in the World during past few decades is the concentration of wealth in a few hands and high inequality.

The proportion of the intermediate manufacturers and the entrepreneurs reduced which led to the fall in employment generation and reduction in purchasing power of the masses. The global capitalists have monopolized and consolidated their power through increased corporate merger and take-over.

The global capitalism emerged during 1980s and the emerging capitalistic class was helped by the young professionals and the managers who manned the growing international production, trade, banking and financial services. The bureaucrats of the World aligned with the capitalists revealed the business opportunities.

The investors and the bureaucrats are the new allies of the capitalists who are intolerant to failure, uncaring about the poverty and the deprivation, unaware of the complex social realities at the home and abroad. They are conservative in the economic philosophy and the social values. Under the impact of the global capitalists, obsessive self-interest has become not only socially acceptable but also the dominant social value.

Under the influence of the ideology of the liberalization and the globalization with unique characteristics of the speculation and the monopoly, the concept of welfare state is virtually repudiated. The new class virtually changed the face of the World. The investor class, the chief ally of capitalists is highly involved in the maximization of profits through so-called gambling in stock and derivative markets.

The investors are earning much more but doing nothing in the real economy, for the production and the distribution of the goods and services. The elites of the third world, who are doing nothing but just earning profits and dividends, are being co-opted by the capitalists of the industrialized western world.

The integration of national elite with international capitalists was brought about by the multi-national corporations which controlled international finance and technology in which intra-firm and international flow of goods, capital, services and technology played an important role and whose major value addition function was the integration, the organization and the management of the flows.

The global function of capitalism is partial and biased towards the Western World. The capital, technology and management are highly mobile internationally and their elasticity of supply is high but being scarce in total supply, they earn high rents, not available as required, in the poor countries of the East.

In the era of the globalization, labour is also an important input in the process of industrialization. It is large and rapidly growing in the World. In developing nations, the labour force consists mainly of high proportion of the unskilled and semi-skilled personnel but their mobility across the national frontier is limited. The local supply of labour force is high.

In the time of the crisis, the West became short sighted and followed the policy of the protectionism. Promotion to the protectionism could not be a solution to the global problems like economic crisis which has affected whole of the humanity.

In 20th century, globalization under the leadership of the U.S. had left the poor into hot water, leaving them either unemployed or under employed. Globalization had created economic dualism and carved out a section in the society with socio-political elites who accepted the values, more, customs and taboos of the West. They were helped by the international electronic media.

The spread of the cultural influence from the global elites threatened the indigenous values and distorted the national cultures. It led to the partial globalization, national disintegration, economic distress and loss of the cultural moorings operated in mutually reinforcing manner to disintegrate the nation-state.

The growing army of the unemployed persons became prone to arrest their ethnic identities which turned to the religious fundamentalism and resorted to communal violence and a step further into the international terrorism.

Thus, the globalization and the industrialization could not solve the problems of the common people but aggravated the problems because of the partial implementation of the concepts.

The last two decades of the twentieth century witnessed the economic crises in the form of debt crises in the developing world along with the globalization and the industrialization. The highly indebted Latin American nations were unable to re-pay the loans and asked for help.

In 1982, Mexico exploded and declared inability to re-pay its international debt. Such a situation was arisen because of increasing inflation, due to rising current account deficit and loose monetary policies. The problems quickly spread in the rest of the developing world, especially in Latin America.

To counter the situation, macro-economic policies were tightened, as a conditionality of the aids from the IMF and the World Bank. The structural adjustment programmes, ushering in the liberalization and the privatization in the economies, were administered.

The problems in these nations were due to the imprudent Government decisions. The IMF-forced-strengthening of the weak financial system did not help much in recovery, as the financial system remained weak years after the crises were over. The real recovery, in the economies of Latin American nations, was due to a surge of the exports to the U.S. and member nations of the North American Free Trade Agreement.

The debt crises of 1990s and after were different in nature from those of 1980s. In 1990s, the crises were staggered and sequential but not spontaneous. They were the Mexican Crisis 1994, the Asian Crisis 1997, the Russian Crisis 1998, the Brazilian crisis 1999 and the Argentine Crisis 2002. They were caused by the short-term commercial bank-debt and the capital market investments.

The Asian crisis was different from others, as in Asia the Government was prudent and the main culprit was the private sector which was imprudent. Therefore, remedy of the Asian

Crisis and other crises should have been different but the IMF and the World Bank prescribed the same remedy, the observance of the fiscal austerity.

Mexican Crisis, 1994

In the Spanish language the crisis is called–'el error de diciembre'–'The December Mistake'. 'The sudden reversal of the former administrative policies of tight currency controls' was the mistake which precipitated into the crisis in Mexico in 1994.

There was a high current account deficit amounting almost 7 percent of the GDP due to the increased expenditures, in the light of the ensuing election. The deficit was to be financed, so the Government issued 'Tesobonos' a type of debt instrument. Investors in 'Tesobonos' sold back it rapidly due to increasing panic created by the deficit, which depleted already low Central Bank reserve of foreign exchange.

Mexico had the fixed exchange system. The country lacked sufficient foreign exchange. Therefore, national currency, peso was de-valued which triggered the crisis. The decision of de-valuation was economically coherent but the way it was handled was the politically incorrect. Rapid withdrawal of the foreign investment aggravated the problem.

The U.S. intervened, bought peso in open market and guaranteed US$ 50 billion loan to recover the Mexican economy. The Peso dollar ratio, 6 peso/dollar, was stabilized. By the turn of the century, the economy gathered momentum with 7 percent economic growth rate.

Asian Crisis, 1997

The East-Asian industrialized nations had de-regulated their financial and capital markets by the early 1990s under the international pressure, in spite of their high savings rate of more than 30 percent. The result of the de-regulation was inflow of the short-term capital which sought the highest return in the next day, next week or next month as opposed to the long-term investment in things like factories etc. where return comes after laps of the gestation period.

The benefits of the industrialization in the East-Asian countries were invested in the capital market and the real estate, not in the real economy for further expansion of industries. Therefore, the economy was volatile.

In early 1990s, the U.S. had recovered from the savings and loan debacle of 1987. In the U.S., Federal Reserve began to raise interest rates to head off the inflation. The U.S. became more attractive destination for the investment in comparison to the 'East-Asian Tigers' and the value of the dollar started increasing to which many of the Asian currencies were pegged. The appreciating currencies made the Asian exports less competitive.

At the same time, China implemented a number of export-oriented reforms which effectively competed with other Asian exporters. The Western importers found Chinese goods cheaper as whose currency was depreciating in relation to the dollar. Availability of large quantity of credit generated high leveraged economic conditions and pushed up the assets prices to an unsustainable level in the East-Asian nations.

During mid-1990s, the maintenance of fixed-exchange rates of currencies encouraged external borrowings, giving exposure to the foreign exchange risk in both the financial and the corporate sectors. The assets prices eventually began to collapse and at the same time the export growth of these nations slowed down dramatically in 1996, deteriorating the current account deficit. The collapse of the assets value caused individual and companies to default on the debt obligation.

Withdrawal of the investment and the credit from the crisis-hit countries was due to the increased panic among the lenders. It resulted into the credit crunch and further developed into the bankruptcy. The exchange market got flooded with the currencies of the crisis-hit countries because of withdrawal by the investors. The foreign investors withdrew in foreign currencies mainly in the dollars.

The depreciative pressure was mounting on their exchange rates. The Governments were forced to raise the domestic interest rates too exceedingly to save the currency values from the collapse. The high internal interest rates damaged the already fragile domestic economy.

Buying up of the excessive domestic currencies by the Governments depleted the foreign exchange reserves of the Central Banks. The fixed exchange rates could no longer sustain the onslaught of the crisis, in the economies of the 'Asian Tigers'.

The currencies were allowed to float and they got depreciated. Consequently, the foreign currency denominated liabilities grew substantially, in domestic currency terms, causing more bankruptcies and deepened the crisis.

The debt crisis, initially resulted into the currency slumping and devaluation. It also caused the slumping of the stock-market and other assets price and precipitous rise in the private debts.

Almost all the East, South-East and South Asian nations suffered from the losses of demand and confidence at the varying degree. The most affected countries were Indonesia, South Korea and Thailand. Hurt by the slumping currency were Hong Kong, Malaysia, Laos and Philippines. The less affected ones were China, India, Taiwan, Singapore, Brunei and Vietnam.

The crisis first began in Thailand with the inflow of the short-term capital which helped to fuel an unsustainable real-estate-boom. The burst of real-estate-boom resulted in the crisis which was mainly the real estate driven. The same type of situation occurred in Malaysia as well.

The economies of the 'Asian Tigers' began to recover by the close of the second millennium, in 1999. The economic growth in these nations, during last quarter of the twentieth century, was due to the State protection along with the capital investment.

The growth was only in productivity. The 'total factor productivity' had increased marginally or not at all. It is the 'total factor productivity' which brings long-term prosperity, not the capital investment to realize high rate of return.

Asian crisis was not regional as hundreds of billions of dollar of the West were at stake. IMF came at the front to bail-out the economies. In the process of bails-out, the IMF was more interested in the making currency, banking and financial systems of these countries as much like as those of the U.S. and Europe.

The pre-condition of the support of the IMF and the World Bank was 'Americanize the institutions' first then borrow to intensify them from the IMF or the World Bank. The financial systems were to be made the transparent to provide a kind of reliable financial information, to be used in the West, to make the sound financial decisions.

When 'Asian Tigers' fell into the crisis in 1997 and asked for support the IMF imposed a conditionality of the 'observance of the fiscal austerity' which was nothing but preparation of balanced budget and tighter monetary policy.

The IMF was delivering the same medicine to each ailing nations. Unlike Latin American nations, Asian nations were already running with the budget surplus, the tight monetary policy and the low-inflation.

In Asia, the problem was with the private sector where the bankers and the borrowers were gambling on the real-estate-bubble. The financial austerity was unable to revive the East-Asian economy because high interest rates were devastating the highly indebted East-Asian firms causing more bankruptcies and the default.

In Latin America, the problem was with the imprudent Government decisions, where fiscal austerity was not being observed. Failure of the IMF policies became evident even then the IMF did not heed.

The economies of these nations were shrinking because of the reduced Government-expenditure. The IMF was demanding balancing of the budget at the time of the recession. Relaxed currency flow restrictions, encouraged by the IMF, produced massive capital flight, which occurred, for instance, in Indonesia.

The IMF demands were:

1. Reduction in the Government expenditure.
2. Reduction in the current account deficit.
3. Increase in the interest rate.
4. Allow to insolvent banks and financial institutions to fail.
5. Restoration of the confidence in the fiscal policy of State.

Countries after countries fell into the crisis. Loans in the dollars became more expensive with respect to the local currency, creating a situation of inability to re-pay to the creditors.

The policy of the 'Structural Adjustment Packages' was contractionary in the nature and was against the traditional Keynesian response in the recession, according to which during the recession, policy should be as follows:

1. Increase in the Government expenditure.
2. Prop-up major companies.
3. Lower the interest rates.

The U.S. pursued the expansionary policy when entered in the recession in 2001, in contrast to the contractionary policy advocated by the IMF. The U.S. lowered the interest rates, increased the Government expenditure and cut the taxes.

The effects of the 'Structural Adjustment Packages' were mixed and their impact controversial. There were needs of such reforms as recommended by the IMF but most of the countries which involved themselves in such policies ended up under-going almost complete political and the financial re-structuring, suffering from

1. Permanent currency devaluation.
2. Massive number of bankruptcies.
3. Collapse of once boomed economies.
4. Real estate bubble-burst.
5. Higher unemployment and social unrest.

The IMF was criticized for encouraging the developing, third world countries of Asia to follow the path of the liberalization in the financial sector which included:

1. Elimination of the restrictions on the capital flow.
2. Maintenance of high domestic interest rates in order to suck in portfolio investment and the bank capital.
3. Pegging up a national currency to the dollar to re-assure foreign investor against the currency risk.

In other words, the IMF itself was the cause of the Asian crisis. Outside the developing world the crisis hit severely the economies of the U.S. and Japan, though they did not collapse.

The most important impact of the Asian crisis was the establishment of harmony between the U.S. and Japan after a gap of five decades which were drifted apart during the Second World War when the U.S. had dropped atomic bombs on Japan in 1945.

In China, the foreign investments were in the form of the long-term, mostly in the factories rather than in short-term investments in securities which insulated it from the rapid capital flight, unlike many of other Asian nations where the foreign capital investments were in the securities, the short-term investments.

The macro-level effects of the crisis were:

1. Sharp reduction in values of the currencies, stock-market and assets.
2. In several Asian countries there was fall in GDP, in terms of the dollar.
3. Many businesses collapsed and millions of the people fell below the poverty line in 1997-98.
4. Surfacing up of the political upheavals.
5. General rise in the anti-Western sentiments.
6. Heavy U.S. investment in Thailand replaced the European investment.
7. Within East, South-East and South Asia the bulk of the investment and significance of economic weight shifted from Japan and (ASEAN) Association of South East Asian

Nations to China and India.

8. The separatist movements intensified in South-East Asia due to the weakening of the central authorities.

The global investors became reluctant to invest in the developing third world countries leading to the economic slow down. The crisis in general was part of a global backlash against the 'Washington Consensus' and the institutions such as the IMF and the World Bank which became unpopular in the third world, mainly in the Asian nations.

Anti-globalization sentiments arisen in the West were evident by the 'anti-globalization movement' manifested in WTO conference of 1999 at Seattle. The World became more assertive towards the regional and the bilateral free-trade agreements as an alternative to the global institutions. Brazil, Russia and India along with many other Asian nations began to copy the Japanese model of weakening their currencies, restructuring their economies so as to create a current account surplus to build large foreign reserve. It led to an ever increasing funding for the U.S. treasury bonds. It paved the path for the stock-market bubble during 1996-2000 and the real estate and housing bubble during 2000-05 in the U.S.

Russian Crisis, 1998

In the spring and the summer of 1998 the Asian crisis spread beyond East-Asia and reached in Russia. The fall in oil prices partly caused the economic crisis in Russia.

The wall of Berlin was fallen in 1989 and USSR was disintegrated in 1991. In the changed atmosphere the Russian economy was to be transformed from the closed to the open one. The two ideologies surfaced up regarding the transition of the Russian economy.

For the Nobel laureates Joseph Stiglitz and Kenneth Arrow, the scholars of one group, in the market economy the institutional infra-structures, like the legal structures that enforce the contracts and the regulatory structures that make a financial system to work, are very important.

These Nobel laureates were aware of the Chinese strategy of the transition which was suitable for the Russian economy as the both were opened from the closed economic system. They emphasized on the importance of the competition rather than just the privatization of the state owned industries. They favoured gradual transition into the market economy.

The other group of scholars consisted of macro-economists who had little knowledge of the history of the Russian economy and relied on the universal facts. For them, the institutions, the history or even the distribution of the income and the wealth simply did not matter.

It is universally accepted that the shock therapy works for the countries in transition to the market economy. This school of thought won the battle and led to the transition of Russia into the market economy in its leadership.

Russian voters rejected the reformers in the 1993 General Election. Strobe-Talbot, then in-charge of non-economic aspects of the Russian policy, admitted that Russia had received "too much shock and too little therapy". All the shocks could not transit the Russian economy into the real market economy at all.

The U.S. and the IMF urged Moscow for the rapid privatization which was to help the virtual plundering of the nation, by a group of the oligarch, in absence of the institutional infrastructure essential for the market-economy.

Anatoly Chubias was the chief architect of Russia's privatization in mid-1998 when the crisis engulfed the Russian economy with falling oil prices. It was a great set-back to the Russian reform and the confidence of the people in free market too.

Because of the increasing inequality of the income and the wealth, the progresses made till then were reversed. After the oil price rise, the long resisted Rubble de-valuation helped the Russian economy to gain some footings.

The story of the developed world during the second half of the twentieth century is something different. After the Second

World War the U.S. economy was the strongest one. The ruined economies of Europe and Japan were gathering momentum. The western capitalist economy had unprecedented and uninterrupted growth up to 1965 which provided a favourable environment to other economies of the World as well.

After 1965, the global economic growth could not sustain. The high economic growth before 1965 was due to the fast recovery of the global economy after the Second World War. To the given level of the technological development, the western capitalist economy got stabilized by late 1960s.

The newly liberated nations of Asia and Africa, after their independence, imported from the West which by mid-1960s slowed down because of the worsening balance of payment situations. The emerging markets of the third world provided a platform for the growth of the export-led economies of the first world. For instance, the auto-industry of the U.S. saw the boom during 1950s and 1960s as 90 percent of the world automobile market was under the control of the U.S.

By 1965, the capitalist system acquired a qualitative change. The production system was broken up into the horizontal and the vertical segments and it was spread world-wide through the multinational corporations which controlled the most advanced technologies as well.

The post-1965 production system was global in nature with the use of new instruments like-transfer pricing, over and under invoicing of traded commodities, intra-corporate trade in the multinational corporations across national boundaries and so on. It influenced the international flow of commodities, technology and capital.

The multinational corporations controlled the international production and determined the global prices of goods and services. In this way, they dominated all types of the markets such as the international, national or local.

During 1960s, the recovering European and the Japanese economies posed stiff competition to the U.S. The U.S. trade deficit started rising as well as the productivity started declining. The global economic system which was running smoothly entered into a phase of a crisis, in which the multinational corporations launched a fresh offensive on the developing world of enforcing new investment priorities which re-shaped their production system and altered their national priorities.

The multinational corporations exploited the vulnerability of the developing countries and pushed them into an external debt, dependency on the foreign technology and the enslaved consumption pattern. Further, development of the nations became subject to the re-deployment of the foreign capital and the technology which were used as the political instruments to control the third world.

During 1970s, the economic growth became stagnant with high inflation and the increasing unemployment along with spreading consumerism. The U.S. de-linked the dollar from the gold standard, so that currency became fluctuating in the new system.

To hedge the currency against the fluctuations concept of derivative re-emerged on the surface. The oil shock of 1973 was a great jolt to the stock-market. The Americans lost their confidence in the stock-market and started investment in the gold, sliver or any valuable metal and the real estate. It did not help the economic growth rather blocked the capital in the form of the non-performing assets.

The U.S. President Ronald Reagan and the liberal Prime Minister of U.K. Margaret Thatcher tried to fight the problem of stagnation and inflation with the industrial recession and the unemployment by withdrawing the State from the economic activities. For them, the best way to manage the economy was 'not to manage that'. They followed a path of the liberalization and the privatization. The private capitals were strengthened through the privatization and restoration of the market forces.

During 1970s, the Japanese economy was booming whereas that of the U.S. was passing through the phase of stagnation. The second oil shock of 1979 was another blow to the already stagnant economy of the U.S.

The de-regulation of the financial market which began in 1970s was supposed to be the very important force of increasing the economic growth in the West. The third world countries were forced to open their economies as the U.S. was doing so.

The U.S. economy was highly tilted towards supply side which assisted the internationalization and the globalization of the production, distribution, technology and the capital. The national markets got integrated with the international market, globalizing the financial operations. The information system and the cultural values became global as well. The capital investment was global but in stock and share markets only, not in the real economy.

The Savings and Loan crisis in the U.S. in 1987 led to the losses which were result of the unmanaged gap between the assets and the liability. It led to the interest rate exposures, speculative investments in junk bonds and service industries, fraud and massive losses from lending to and investing in the U.S. commercial and the real estate sector.

In 1970s, the de-regulation of the U.S. interest rate and inflation created a volatile interest rate market. In 1980s, the Savings and Loan industry failed to tackle the risk inherent in funding of the long-term, fixed interest mortgages by means of the short-term deposits. A gap was opened up between liabilities, i.e., the short-term deposits and the short-term interest rates and assets, i.e., the income generated by the long-term, fixed-rate mortgages and the re-payments.

The value of existing Savings and Loan portfolios moved higher because of the increasing interest rates. At the same time the value of the long-term low interest rate residential mortgages was low, consequently, insolvency increased.

Around 1990, the assets price collapsed in Japan which had an extra-ordinary deflationary effect on what was the World's the most dynamic economy of the day.

In 1989, the Wall of Berlin was fallen and in 1991 USSR was disintegrated. The collapse of USSR and its control over the East European countries dismantled the COMECOM Trade Agreement and the Warsaw Pact. The effect of these events was that the World became univocal under the leadership of the U.S.

In 1990s, the U.S. de-regulation of the financial market was continued as a catalyst to the growth and the productivity. The explosive growth of the un-regulated derivatives took place during the period. The interest rate was low which made easy availability of the money.

In the age of the computer and high developed technology, the American economy flourished. During the period of the President Clinton the confidence of the people of the U.S. returned in the stock-market which grew more than three fold. The roaring stock market boom was called the dot-com-boom.

The Dot-com or the Information Technology Boom was a speculative bubble between 1995 and 2001, with climax on March 10, 2000 when the NASDAQ peaking at 5132.52 points.

The rapid growth of the stock-market was due to rapid growth in the internet sector and related fields, marked by founding of new internet based companies. Low interest rate in 1998-'99 infused money in public which was invested in the stock-markets, so the stocks got shoot up. It was a boom like other historical booms such as:

- Railway boom 1840s
- Automobile and Radio boom 1920s
- Transistor Electronics boom 1950s
- Computer time-sharing boom 1960s
- Home Computers and
- Bio-technology boom 1980s
- Dot-com or stock-market or
- High-tech boom 1990s

The dot-com-boom was based on the internet companies whose survival depended on the expansion of their customers.

In 1999-2000 the Federal Reserve had increased the internet (tax) rates six times. The bubble got burst on March 10th, 2000. Microsoft Company was declared monopolistic by the Federal Court. The poor results of the Internet retailers and the increased rates of the internet caused the burst of the boom.

By turn of the 20th century, the World was divided into two parts viz. the first world and the third world as the second world was melted away with the disintegration of USSR into 15 independent States, in 1991. The successor States of former USSR formed Commonwealth of Independent States.

Now The World was divided into 2 groups. One group, led by the U.S. was industrialized consisting of North America, the Western Europe and their off-shoots, Australia-New Zealand and Japan.

The other group was a conglomeration of the industrializing and the developing nations of Eastern Europe, Commonwealth of Independent States (the successor States of erstwhile USSR), Asia, Africa, Latin America and Oceania. The big economies of this group are China, India, Russia, Brazil and the industrialized nations of East-Asia.

With the expansion of the industrialization outside America, Europe and Japan, the industrial economies with different strength emerged in the other parts of the World. America and Europe formed core area during the colonial period. Now the core was expanding with the emergence of other economic powers in Asia and Latin America and the periphery was reducing.

The colonial core-periphery model weakened as the nations were no longer tied to U.K. or the U.S. The significant feature was highly increased role of the multinational corporations which controlled almost every aspect of the economy. The nations of East-Asia entered into the industrialized club during 1970s and 1980s.

After the Asian Crisis the significance of China and India got increased. The two nations with high population were semi-industrialized at the close of the century. Full industrialization of India and China means industrialization of more than one third of the World.

Thus, the emergence of China and India in the world economic scene had shifted the centre of gravity of the development and economic performance from the West to the East and from the North to the South, at the close of the second millennium.

9

Dawn of the Third Millennium

The World, at the time of the beginning of the third millennium, was well knit due to the expanding communication and information technology. The computer networking played significant role in spreading the information. The global networking of the computer is called-the Internet (international networking) and that of the local area is called-LAN (local area networking).

The swifter and the global availability of the information made the World a Global Village. The multi-national corporations governed the production and the distribution system of the World along with the technology transfer and the capital flow. The consumerism was spreading throughout the World.

The hundreds of years old pattern of the trade between the Western Europe and the Northern America weakened. The trade system is deeply rooted in 'the market system at the gross root level' where the poor buyers laid the foundation of the global trade. The global capitalists get the benefit from such a system. The global trade system entered into the crisis due to the falling of the purchasing power in the masses which led the fall in demand of goods and services.

Conglomerations of the industrializing and the developing nations of Eastern Europe, Commonwealth of Independent States (the successor States of erstwhile USSR), Asia, Africa, Latin America and Oceania were emerging. The big economies of this group are China, India, Russia, Brazil and the industrialized nations of East-Asia.

China and India are the two most populous countries in the World. With such a large population base more than five percent growth rate over long period is a good indicator of the development. The nations with smaller population size might have grown at faster rate but were not much significant in the World of almost seven billion people.

One who develops with larger population-base is more important from the global perspective. The whole of the population of the World is to be uplifted not a few people. The nations of the first world made the 'solo vertical flight' in the field of the economic development and the rest of the World remained far behind.

In the early years of the third millennium, almost 40% population of the World is making stride in regard to the development and industrialization under a group called BRIC, consisting of Brazil, Russia, India and China.

Indians have played very important role in the scientific and the technological innovations. China and India have more than one third population of the World. They are the continental and the sub-continental in size and economy with huge markets as well as large local work-force having skilled and unskilled both.

Industrialized China and India will dwarf any other economy of the World. Both the countries are complementary to each other regarding the development. China is stronger in the manufacturing with multi-billion dollar electronics and heavy industrial plants whereas India is stronger in the software design, devices and precision industry.

The multinational corporations are utilizing the capacities of both the nations. The software and circuits are designed in India whereas the manufacturing and the assembling take place in China. India has low cost laboratories and China has low cost factories.

India and China are producing half a million scientists and engineers annually. The U.S. is producing just 60,000 in a year. Heavy weight of India and China are being felt in the field of medicine and daily use materials as well.

Scisco's Schcimmen puts it, "we came to India for cost, we stayed for quality and we are now investing for innovation." The pivotal force of the economy is the middle class, the consumer class, which is rising to drive the changes and innovations in the two nations.

There is rising demand of the latest technologies and consumer items, imitating the American and the Western consumerism. The consumerism was begun in the U.S. in 1970s. Both the countries have become leaders, from the followers, in the field of the consumer electronics.

In India, information technology services industry is successful. India has sophisticated manufacturing know-how. Tata Steel is among the World's the most efficient producers. India has several top precision auto parts companies like Bharat Forge Limited, the World's biggest supplier of the Chassis parts to the major auto makers. Thus, in the early years of the third millennium China and India spearheaded as the emergent stronger economic powers with the stable growth rate.

In the early years of 21st century, in 2008, the World GDP (the value of all final goods and services produced in a given year), according to the World Bank Report was 69.70 trillion dollars measured in the terms of the purchasing power parity which takes into account the relative cost of living and the inflation rates of the countries, rather than using just the exchange rates which may distort the real differences in income.

The top ten economies of the World, in 2008, GDP measured in trillion dollars at PPP, were the U.S. (14.20), China (7.90), Japan (4.35), India (3.39), Germany (2.92), Russia (2.29), United Kingdom (2.18), France (2.11), Brazil (1.98) and Italy (1.84). Thus, the second, the third and the fourth economies of the World are the Asian and share of BRIC nations (Brazil, Russia, India and China) in global GDP is (15.56) more than 20 percent. The share of the U.S. economy is almost 20 percent and that of Euro zone (10.90) in the World GDP is about 15 percent.

At this point of time, in the first decade of the 21st century, the World is divided into the two distinct groups. One headed by the U.S. is fully industrialized but highly dependent on the outer world for the market. Other has two highly populous and big economies with huge national markets. The conspicuous feature of the 21st century is Asia-centric development of the World with emphasis on the welfare of the people.

Price-rise and Food Security

The price of a commodity and purchasing power of the mass determine the pace and the direction of the economic activities in a society. The low commodity-price and the high purchasing power indicate good health of the economic activities and the boom in it.

The purchasing power in a society is created by the savings and the borrowings. The high purchasing power, created by either of the way or by both of the ways, brings consumerism in a society. For instance, in the U.S. society the consumerism was swelled up by the increased earnings of the people supported by the borrowings.

In the early years of the 21st century, the consumerism in the Indian and the Chinese society was increased due to the savings and the financing of the consumer durables by the banking and non-banking institutions. The reduction in the savings takes place due to the reduction in the earnings or increase in the prices of the commodities or due to both.

The price of a commodity is determined by the cost of the production and the marginal profit of the manufacturer. The high profit, taken by a manufacturer and others, results in the concentration of the wealth in a few hands. It increases prices of the goods and sucks money from the masses and reduces purchasing power of the masses. The masses are left with less money for other products to be purchased.

At a given level of money in hands of the people, either by earnings and savings or by borrowings, rising prices of the commodities bring down the purchasing power of the masses which reduces the sale of the commodities as well. Thus, a vicious circle of less demand, less production and slowed business activities is created and further economic operations lose their momentum giving rise to a recession in an economy.

The producers, in an economy, can maintain sustainable level of sale and purchase of the products by taking less profit and keeping the prices low. The present day crisis, through which the World is passing, is a result of the decreasing demand of the goods and the services because of the low buying capacity of the masses.

The distribution and re-distribution of the wealth and income, during the last five centuries, have created a cleavage in the World and have divided the people into 'haves' and 'have-nots'. The 'haves' have accumulated too much wealth whereas the 'have-nots' have left with almost nothing to buy the products of the 'haves'. The 'haves' have grabbed the wealth of the 'have-nots' through the different means and mechanisms of the market. Therefore, the products of the 'haves' are unable to be purchased in the market of 'have-nots' by them, in absence of the purchasing power.

The wealth of the 'haves' have not come from the heaven rather it has come from the 'have-nots'. If the poor don't have money, the rich can't multiply their wealth through trade and business. It is the poorest person who is the foundation stone of the prosperity of the rich. In the time of crises the rich are more affected than the poor because the poor are adept to live in the deprivation, to which the rich are not. The poor are lying on the ground and have no chance of falling but the rich are falling, as they are unable to maintain the required level which is done by the purse of the poor.

The first decade of the 21st century witnessed a commodity-price-boom started in the previous century. In the beginning of the boom, the oil-prices rose world-over due to the increased oil demand, led by the economic development in different parts of the World and the decreasing oil-supply from its peak. Iraq-war affected the production of the oil in the

Middle East which is the main oil-producing region. The inadequate refining capacity abated the problem as well because the crude oil could not be refined as much as required.

The U.S along with China and India created the maximum demand. The U.S. tried to off-set the excess demand of oil by using ethanol. The U.S. accelerated the production of the ethanol, a bio-fuel prepared from the corn which is a crop on which the pigs are grown in the U.S.

Up to 2005, Brazil was the largest producer of the ethanol in the World. After wards, the U.S. took the place of Brazil in the production of the ethanol. Bio-fuels are mixed with fossil fuels and used as additives. Demand for bio-ethanol increased in 1990s when it was found that methyl tertiary butyl ether, (MTBE), an oxygenate additive in gasoline, was contaminating ground water.

The bio-fuel in the U.S. was invented in early years of 20th century but interest in the commercial use increased after second oil shock of 1979. Since 2002 demand for ethanol, as an additive in gasoline, increased, almost at the same time when oil prices were rising significantly.

The corn is the main feed-stock of the both, the bio-diesel and the ethanol. Development of the cellulosic bio-fuel is on the way but its cost is higher than corn based bio-fuel at the present level of the technology.

Ethanol industry changed the crop-combination and the cropping pattern in the U.S. The farming of corn had become more profitable as its prices were rising due to the use in the ethanol industry. Now it is a cash crop. The area under staple crops shrank and that of the corn expanded. Thus, the production of rice, wheat, soybeans and so on reduced due to the decrease in the area under such crops in the U.S.

The exclusive land deals for production of corn, for the ethanol, in developing nations were made. Along with other natural and cultural factors, it caused food grain shortage. Ethanol, an energy-intensive alternative, is a long-term option which is not an immediate solution to the energy needs.

Indirectly, the bio-fuel affected the production and cost of the animal based food products. The food shortage resulted in the price-rise of the food grains in the world market.

With the economic development and enriched dietary habits, the demand of meat increased in both, the developed and the developing world. More production of the meat required more fodder for the live stocks. The prices of the fodder also increased due to its diversion for ethanol. The high price of the fodder led the price-rise of beef, pork, milk and other dairy products.

The cost of fertilizers got increased due to the high petroleum prices which added and abated the price rise of the food grains, fodder, fruits and vegetables as well. The prices of the oil along with almost every edible and non-edible material got stabilized at higher rate.

The rise in price was not painful in the U.S. and other developed world but it was very much painful to the poor people, in the poor countries. The U.S. cut back food aids to the under-nourished nations of Africa by 41 percent, because of the high food prices and triple demands of the food grains for the food, fodder and ethanol.

The main sufferers of the price rise were the poor. Some were unable to buy even the food material and some could buy the food materials only and nothing was left with them for their other requirements. The population which had crossed the poverty line dipped again into the deep poverty because of the price-rise.

The boom in the commodity price ended with the slowdown in the global economy. Before the slowdown, the purchasing power in the poor countries was already low. The slowdown reduced the purchasing power of the rich in the developed countries too. So, the burst of the real-estate-boom and slowdown in the economy along with the commodity-price-boom led to the demand destruction and the purchasing power crisis in the World.

During the commodity-price-boom between 2003 and

2008, the prices of oil rose by 320 percent in the dollar terms and that of the internationally traded food material by 138 percent. After mid-2008 prices of the oil and food material declined sharply. The socio-economic effects of the price-rise still continue and the prices are still higher than those of 1990s.

A new World Bank Report-Global Economic Prospect-2009 published on December 9, 2008, illustrates, in an article titled Commodity Price Boom ends with slowing global growth, that "High commodity prices, particularly of food, have had a profound impact on poverty, pushing 130 to 155 million people below the poverty line just between December 2005 and December 2007. The worst impact was in urban areas. While Government policies reacted swiftly to off-set the worst effects of the higher prices, many of these efforts were poorly targeted and expansive."

It again emphasized, "Action is also needed at the global level to discourage export bans of food grains, strengthen agencies like World Food Programmes and improve information about the co-ordination of existing domestic grain reserves."

A dignified human life can't be achieved without fulfilling the basic needs of food, clothing and shelter. Even the mere survival of the human being is not possible without the food. According to the Report of Food and Agricultural Organization 2003, about 852 million people were hungry and had to live on in-sufficient food availability.

The financial crisis which began in 2007 brought about 150 million more people in the band of the hungry ones who had to live below the lowest poverty line. There are different poverty lines in different nations. For instance, in the U.S. poverty line is defined as US$ 10 per day per person and extreme poverty line is US$ 1.25 per day per person.

Almost 2 billion people in the World are suffering from the food problems and the food-insecurity intermittently. Almost half of the World's population, nearly 3.3 billion, lived in urban areas as on November 2007. Any disruption in the economic system is first reflected in the urban poor. It is the class which usually crosses poverty line and reverts back in the band of the poor and hungry at the time of a crisis.

When the problems arise in the system like less production or increase in the prices of the food material or any other crisis, the urban poor becomes the first victim. The rise in commodity prices had adversely affected the food security of the urban poor in particular and the poor in general.

The food in-security of the people is basically a politico-economic problem. It is less concerned to the production of the food material. Availability of food materials, prices and purchasing power determine the food security of the people. The price rise had made the less availability of the food to almost 150 million people. The food production, purchasing power and locally available food material are more important.

The World is divided into the two groups, viz. the developed and the developing ones. In the developed world agriculture is a commercial activity and it is called-'agribusiness' and is characterized by the high production, high productivity, involvement of the big machines, less manual labour and the subsidized high capital.

Agribusiness is done by the multinational corporations and is a capital intensive venture. Much of its produce goes to the processing industry and a little goes in the market unprocessed. The processed food is supplied world over maximizing the profits of the producers.

In the developing world farming is not an industry but a way of life for farmers. It is for the subsistence and a full-time job for almost all the family members. Farming in such a region is characterized by the low production, low productivity, less mechanization, less capital investment and high manual labour. The agricultural produce is directly consumed without undergoing in the food processing industry.

It is the region where population is more and food production is less. Starvation prevails and shortage of food material exists which is supplemented by the food-aid programmes. On the earth there are one to two billion people who are starving regularly or intermittently. The starvation of the people is to be wiped out, for making the earth prosperous and sustainable.

The average global development is much more but there are regional variations. The globalization has integrated the elites of the nations but not the poor of the nations. There is urgent need for active participation of more than 6 billion people living on the earth in a global economy. There is a large population which does not have proper and regular employment.

The U.S., the IMF, the World Bank and the liberalized financial markets, over the globe, could not bring much of the population above the poverty line, making them active participants in the global economy, in last couple of decades. Even the most trivial need, the food, of billions of people could not be fulfilled.

The policies of the West followed for the East was neither in the interest of the West nor in that of the East. The Eastern poor nations were persuaded by the rich Western nations for changing the land-use pattern, i.e., diversion of the land for those products which were not produced in the West, mainly tropical plantation products. They were advised to import the food grains for themselves and to produce local crops on their own land for the West.

The poor countries couldn't be uplifted from the poverty by imported food material. They need the self -sufficiency and the self-reliance in the food material and the food production, to fulfil their needs according to the local preferences.

The self-sufficiency in the food production and the agriculture are not isolated phenomena, as in the East the agriculture is an economy of the people. The agricultural development is needed for the all round socio-economic development of the people.

In such a society the agricultural development will bring the self-sufficiency in the food production, job opportunity for youth and the holistic development of the agrarian society as a whole. Thus, the food production and the agrarian development, in the third world, are very crucial for the sustainable earth.

The West did not attack on the roots of problem in the developing world through poverty eradication programmes. It tried to solve the problem of the poor nations as a by-product of the process of the maximization of profit of the multi-national corporations.

One of the major hurdles in the self-sufficiency and the food sovereignty in the developing world is the subsidized diversion of the land under food grains to the ethanol production. It has been one of the causes of the food shortage in the early years of 21st century. In the U.S maize conversion into the ethanol increased by 4 times between 2003 and 2009.

Some Governments and the multinational corporations are buying rights of agricultural land for agribusinesses and the long-term perspective. In the name of the contract business local people are doing farming on their own land for the outsider bosses. The farmers are hungry because they are not producing what is required to them but they are producing what is required to others.

South Korean firm Daewoo Logistics secured farmland in Madagascar to grow maize and crops for bio-fuel. Oil rich investors are looking for agricultural lands in Sudan, Ethiopia, Ukraine, Kazakhstan, Pakistan, Cambodia and Thailand for the commercial agriculture.

The tropical agricultural resources which are not found in the West are being exploited by the multinational corporations in their interest. They are buying rights of doing agriculture in the tropics for the tropical products for selling in the industrialized world.

The productive agricultural lands in tropics is going into the hands of the multinational corporations whereas the poor and less fertile land remains in the hands of the local farmers on which they have to perform farming for themselves.

The local people are marginalized in the production and productivity. Through land deals the multinational corporations are snatching the food sovereignty of the local people. The multinational corporations supported by the global institutions are supposed to protect the interests of the poor.

The concept of the food sovereignty revolves around the business practices of the multinational corporations who are following the neo-colonial business practices. The poor nations of tropics have become the dumping ground of the subsidized food products of the West, produced under agribusinesses which are hampering the self-sufficiency and the self-reliance in the food-production in the tropics.

Therefore, it is advocated that production of the cash crop in the impoverished nations should be banned so as the local farmers could concentrate on the subsistence crops.

Sufficient food is produced globally but there are cases of the starvation in the World. To ensure food to all the people food justice is required. It is an economic approach to improve food security in the developing world.

In the centre of the food problem is "what is lacking is not food material but the political will to fairly distribute food regardless of the recipient's ability to pay." Basic goal is that no one should live without enough food because of the economic constraints or the social inequality.

According to (FAO) Food and Agricultural Organization Report 2003, there were 22 countries out of which 16 were in Africa where the under-nourishment prevalence rate was over 35 percent. But 60 percent people were in Asia and only 25 percent in Africa. The proportion of the affected ones in respect to the total population was higher in Africa, about 53 percent whereas it was only 16 percent in Asia.

The impoverished people come from the different backgrounds but the agriculture in any forms is the economic background for most of them. Hunting and gathering which is rarely a type of farming is also background for some of the poor in the World. The different types of the agriculture may be slash-and-burn farming, sedentary-tillage farming, subsistence farming or pastoralism i.e., an animal husbandry which is also a form of agriculture.

The Americanization and the Westernization of the people is against the cultural ethos of these people. The people should be allowed to develop themselves according to their genius, local need, culture and values. Their sovereignty and freedom in performing agriculture and in selection of what is to be grown in their land should be kept in their hands.

The people should gradually be brought into the global-mainstream after making them the self-reliant and the self-sufficient in fulfilling of their basic needs of food, clothing and shelter. Precisely, what are required for them are- there is a need to:

1. meet the food needs of low income nations;
2. build food reserves in the poor countries to meet their own needs;
3. develop sustainable food production and distribution system in their local commodities and countries;
4. develop ability and make the individual the self-reliant in fulfilling their own food needs; and
5. develop local agriculture and agro-based economic activities.

Food problem in the World is mainly due to the political reasons rather than apolitical ones. There are examples in last century that the food problems arose because the Governments undermined the food security in their own nations. International undermining of the food security has sometimes caused food problems also. In most cases, the Government has been responsible for the food problem.

In the 21st century, priority is sustainable holistic development of the World as a unit. It could not be achieved without the balanced regional development which could only be achieved by eradicating the poverty and the food problem from the earth. The major problem is how actively the State should manage the economy and provide public services to tackle the problem of the poverty.

FAO defines the food security, "to all people at all time, physical and economic access to sufficient, safe and nutritional food to meet their dietary needs and food preferences for an active and healthy life."

"Former U.S. President Bill Clinton told to a U.N. gathering on October 16th, 2008, "The global food crisis shows, we all blew it including me by treating food crops, 'like colour T.V.' instead of as a vital commodity for World's poor"...Clinton criticized decades of policy making by World Bank, the IMF and others encouraged by the U.S. that pressured Africans in particular into dropping Government subsidies for fertilizers, improved seeds and other farm input as a requirement to get aid.

Africa's self-sufficiency declined and food imports rose. Now sky rocketing prices in the international grain trade, on an average more than doubling between 2006 and 2008, have pushed many in poor countries deeper into poverty."

"Food is not commodity like others. We should go back to a policy of maximum food self-sufficiency. It is crazy for us to think we can develop countries around the World, without increasing their ability to feed themselves."—Bill Clinton, October16th, 2008.

Thus, the first step to the development of the World is the national food self sufficiency which could only be achieved by concerted efforts by the World community as a whole. All nations, the poor or the rich, have to come forward to boost the food self- sufficiency in the poor nations.

Booms and Crashes

Booms and crashes in the capitalist economy are common features resulting from the structure and the function of the economy. It is the finance sector of the economy which is prone to the booms and crashes not the real sector. The present day global financial system is highly technical and complex. The financial market is a socio-economic formation, organized as regularized and interconnected codified system of individuals and the collective actors.

The finance system is composed of the relations between the individual and the collective actors like dealers in stock-exchange, managers of hedge fund, finance department of the multinational corporations, Central Banks and the Government.

One of the socio-economic actions in the finance system is speculation which is an outcome of the open market along with the monopoly. The speculation has been central in various booms during previous century and differs from the boom to boom. The number of objects of the speculation increases from the beginning to the end of a boom. Greed of speculators for the highest possible profit encourages the investment in the speculation.

Finance-market runs under the philosophy of the finance capitalism which subordinates the production processes with respect to the operations and functions. Finance capitalism gives more weightage to the finance system. It has little to do with real economy or production processes. It is characterized by the pursuit of profits earned from the purchase and sell of the financial products like bonds, stocks, futures and other derivatives. It also encourages investment in currencies and financial products.

The finance capitalism also includes lending of the capital at interest. It is exploitative by nature as it supplies income to non-labourers, i.e., profit makers are not contributing in the real economy, by means of the production of goods and services. The profit makers from the finance system make purchases of the goods and services from the markets without contributing in the production process. Thus, they are creating inflation in the economy.

The industrial capitalism, in contrast to the finance capitalism, earns profit from the manufacturing of goods and services which has passed through the various stages of changes and developments with the changing technology of the mass of production during the last a few centuries. It has provided bed-rock and strength to the global economy.

The 19th century industrial capitalism was organized around the standardized mass production, scale economies and the mass consumption. In 20th century, with the changes in the technology, the orientation of the industrial capitalism changed into the 'flexible' production, innovation, scope economies and the differentiated pattern of the consumption.

The information and communication revolution with the global networking of computers has drastically changed the global scenario. After the computer-revolution, digitalization, electronic information processing technologies and tendencies, the financial and industrial capitalism revolutionized the different processes of the global economy. Significant changes have occurred in the processes of the production, distribution, exchange and so on.

The capitalism, whether it is financial or industrial, in the 21st century, has become disorganized with the decreasing national regulations. The global capitalists and the multi-national companies have monopolized the production of the goods and services. The monopoly of the multinational corporations in the field of the real economy has resulted into the decrease in number of the small and the medium entrepreneurs who have to play very important role in the global economy.

The monopoly of the multinational corporations has contributed in the economy but could not generate the required quantum of the employment. The economic growth took place, the production and the productivity increased but at the same time unemployment also increased. Consequently, the benefits of the growth went in a few hands and caused the concentration of the wealth.

By close of the 20th century, a situation arose in which the huge production with high productivity was achieved in the economy but the masses suffered from the unemployment and under employment. Therefore, they did not have money to purchase the goods and service, even at lower prices, which was produced and dumped by the multinational corporations.

A maxim of Henry Ford, the great industrialist of the U.S. in 20th century, "cars can't buy cars" emphasizes that the buyers are equally important as the producers. If there is no buyer, for whom it is being produced and how will producer realize the cost of production?

During 20th century, demand was subordinated to the supply. The supply side of the economics was properly handled and to increase the supply was the main focus. It was presumed that the supply would automatically create the demand but it did not happen as much desired. The imbalance between the two grew exponentially. Breaking of the balance between demand and supply is called the burst of the boom.

The global economy grew very fast after the Second World War. It got the features like the predominance of the financial sector in the economy and the global spreading of the production processes under the multinational corporations. The processes of the liberalization led to the relaxations in the national rules and regulations mainly in the financial sector.

The conspicuous feature of the era was the declining significance of the middle class entrepreneurs who have been job providers mostly for the semi skilled and unskilled work-force. The economy grew faster but the employment at the snails speed. It adversely affected the demand side of the economics as the purchasing power of the masses did not increase in general. The stock-market became the land mark and the measurement scale of the development and the growth of the economy which undermined the real economy.

In second half of the 20th century, the economy was associated with the various trends and the developments which took place in the U.S., Western Europe and Japan. NASDAQ, a stock-exchange of the U.S. became the symbol of the new global economy, especially in term of its trading form and functions.

By beginning of the 21st century, the first world came

under the problem of the over-production. Its root cause was that the producers did not follow Henry Ford, the leading industrialist of the previous century, whose emphasis was also on the buying capacity of the people. The third world is a bigger market than the first one for them, where virtually no such growth took place to create the purchasing power in masses to buy their products.

In the period of over-production and under-selling, the first world was watching the cycles of the booms and the crashes. After burst of the high-tech or the dot-com-bubble in 2000, the U.S. investors lost their confidence in the stock-market and started investing in the real estate, assuming it the safer investment destination.

Another feature of the western economy which surfaced up during the last quarter of the 20th century was the concept of the derivatives. It greatly transformed the western economy in particular and the global economy in general. By the turn of century, the derivative market got swelled up to a large extent and was gone far ahead to the stock-market. The West successfully maximized the profits through the derivatives in early years of the 21st century.

Derivatives

Derivative is a trading of the future possibilities. It is both a security and a contract. It is a security derived from the underlying like debt instruments, shares, loans (secured or unsecured), risk instruments, contract for difference or any other form of securities. It is a contract which derives its value from the prices or indices of the underlying securities.

In general parlance, derivative is nothing but a bet. Share is also a bet but the difference between the two is that when a person buys stock or share, he owns a part of the company that deals with goods and services and has issued share, so the stock has some intrinsic value. But when a person owns a derivative he owns nothing and even then if he owns anything it is just the future possibilities.

The underlying of the credit derivatives are the loans, bonds or other forms of the credit and the value of the underlying changes with regard to the time and the space.

When the U.S. currency was detached from the gold standard and had become floating in early 1970s, the old concept of the derivative was brought into the operation to hedge the currency against the fluctuations of the currency and interest rate. The hedging of not only currency but that of other things also was done through the derivative contracts.

Hedging is an activity which mitigates the risk of the economic losses from the changes in the value of the underlying. The derivatives were destined to hedge against the financial risks and to make the financial system more stable. But it undermined and destroyed the very system which was to be protected by it.

Black-Scholes model revolutionized the modern finance and gave new life to an old concept, the derivative, into a new format. The model, in association with probability theory, exploited the world of derivatives. The global and local networking of the computer expanded the derivative markets further.

The derivative market is one where if one makes a mistake, it is fatal. Long Term Capital Management (a hedge fund), Baring Orange Country and Enron debacles are some of the examples of what happened when the things went wrong in the derivative market.

The concepts and the practices which prevailed during the different phases in the modern world economic history were:

1. The concept and the practice of the 'lender of the last-resort' in 18th century.
2. The concept of the gold standard in 19th century.
3. The concept of the multi-lateral system of the global financial regulation and the governance in 20th century.
4. The concept of the derivative prevailed during the very early years of the 21st century.

There are different types of the derivatives which are

frequently used in the present day derivative markets. The contracts to buy and sell an asset on or before a future date at a price specified today are called futures and forwards. Options give owners the right but not the obligations to buy and or sell an asset. When parties enter into an option price is specified. Swaps are the contracts to exchange cash on or before a specified future date.

The contracts which are negotiated privately and traded directly between the two parties without going through exchange or any other intermediary are called the over-the-counter (OTC) contracts. The OTC contract market is largely made up of sophisticated parties like the banks and the hedge funds. The OTCs are largely un-regulated disclosures of information between the parties.

The derivatives mainly leverage the debt in an economy. They create even more difficulty for underlying real economy to service its debt obligations and to curtail the real economic activities which can cause a recession in the economy.

The credit default swap is an insurance contract between a protection buyer and a protection seller covering a corporation's (the referenced entity) specific bond or loan. It is an OTC contract and could be sold to another party. The protection buyer pays an upfront amount and an annual premium to the protection seller to cover any loss on the face amount of the referenced bond or loan.

The credit default swaps are not standardized instruments, not securities technically, not transparent, not traded on exchange, not subject to the present securities law, not regulated and so on.

Paul B. Farrel wrote in an article titled- ''Derivatives the new ticking bomb'', on March 10, 2008.

"The fact is derivatives have become world's newest and biggest black market exceeding the illicit traffic in stuff like arms, drugs, alcohols, gambling, cigarettes, stolen art and pirated movies. Why? Because like all black market, derivatives are perfect way of getting rich while avoiding taxes and government regulations. And in today's slowdown plus volatile global market, Wall Street knows derivatives remain a lucrative business."

Recently, Pimco's bond fund king Bill Gross said, "What we are witnessing is essentially the breakdown of our modern day banking system".

Gross says, "We are creating a new shadow banking system. Derivatives are now not just risk management tool. As Gross and others see it the real problem is that derivatives are now a new way of creating money outside the normal central bank liquidity rules. How? The derivatives are private contracts between the two companies or institutions".

"And it takes place out-side normal business channel out there in "free market". That is the wonderful world of derivatives and it is creating massive bubbles that would soon implode."

The derivative market is larger than the entire World's financial wealth because same assets might be involved in the several different derivatives as an underlying. The financial experts have to make an educated guess about the total amount at stake in all these contracts.

The notional value of the Word's Over-the-Counter derivatives at the end of 2007 was US$ 596 trillion, according to Bank of International Settlement. The values of the World's financial assets, including stocks, bonds and bank deposits, were just US$ 167 trillion in 2007, according to McKinsey.

The credit default swap, a derivative based on the credit default and exchange of the money on or before future date, is at the centre of the present financial crisis which grew from US$ 2.69 trillion in 2003 or US$ 54.6 trillion in 2008.

What is happening in both the stock and the credit markets is a direct result of what is playing out in the credit default swap market.

Federal Reserve could not let Bear Stearns to enter into the bankruptcy because the trillions of the dollars of the credit default swaps on its book would be wiped out. All the banks and the institutions that had insurance written by the 'Bear' would not be able to say that they were insured or hedged any more.

What happened to the American Insurance Group? The AIG got greedy. The AIG, as on 30th June, 2008 had written US$ 441 trillion worth of the swaps on the corporate bonds and worse, on the mortgage backed securities. When the value of the insured referenced entities, the corporate bonds and the mortgage-backed securities fell, the AIG had massive write downs and additionally had to post more collateral. When its ratings were down graded the company had to post even more collaterals which it did not have.

The credit default swaps are causing many of the massive write downs at the banks, investment banks and insurance companies. Knowing what it means for the hedge funds and the credit and stock markets is key to understand where it might end and how?

Collateralized mortgage-backed securities are also at the bottom of the present crisis. The frightening truth is that we can't even get to them because they are covered so completely by what one can call the multiplier catalyst credit default swaps.

In the early 1990s, the credit default swap was devised by J.P. Morgan and Company, now J.P. Morgan Chase and Company, in order to hedge their loan risks. Contributory Editor of Investment News:Money Morning, Shah Gilani writes-

"Are you wondering what's really going on in the market? The truth is probably more frightening than your worst fears. And yet you won't hear about it any where else because 'they' can't tell you. 'They' are the U.S. Federal Reserve and the U.S. Treasury Department, they can't tell you what is really going on because there is nothing they can do about it except what they have been trying to do add liquidity."

When Mr. Gilani asked what the economic purpose of swaps was, the answer came back-"to make money for the bank."

Gilani writes, "there are credit default swaps written on sub-prime mortgage securities. It is bad enough that the sub-prime mortgage pools, banks, investment banks, insurance companies, hedge funds bought were over rated and ended up falling precipitously in value as fore-closure mounted on underlying mortgages in the pools".

He further adds, "What is even worse, however, is that speculators sold and bought trillion of dollars insurance that these pools would not default. The sellers of this insurance, for example, AIG, are getting killed as default continues to rise with no end in sight. And this is only where the story begins."

Investor Buffet and Gross warn that US$ 516 trillion derivative bubble is a disaster, waiting to happen. Wall Street did not listen to Buffet. The derivatives grew into a massive bubble, from about US$ 100 trillion in 2002 to 516 trillion dollars by 2007.

The derivative bubble, according to Buffet and Gross, was fuelled by:

1. Sarbanese-Oxley increased corporate disclosure and Government oversight.
2. Sub-prime housing boom created by the U.S. monetary policy.
3. War budget burdened the U.S. Treasury and future entitlement programmes.
4. Trade deficit with China and other destroyed the value of dollar.
5. Oil and commodity rich nation demanding equity payment rather than debt.

The Sarbanes-Oxley Act 2002, an Act of the corporate governance, is one of the important and the significant Acts in the U.S. It is enacted to protect the investors by improving the accuracy and the reliability of the corporate disclosures made pursuant to the securities law and for other purposes. The Act not only provides the additional controls but significantly increases the penalties also. The Act dictates the improved corporate governance and the increased accountability of the officers and the boards of the directors of the publicly traded companies. The indenture of the audit committee must improve and penalties for the corporate misconduct must intensify.

10

Economic Crisis 2008

The response of the low interest rate, in the first decade of the 21st century, was different from that of the 20th century when it had contributed the growth and the productivity in the U.S. After the burst of the dot-com-bubble, the excess funds released from the bubble as well as from the credits were put in the real estate, in the form of the construction of new buildings and renovation of the houses. It gave birth to another bubble in the U.S. economy, the 'housing bubble'.

The real estate speculation was based on the derivatives. The future possibilities of the mortgage-backed securities were traded, sold and re-sold in the derivative markets. The mortgages taken by the individuals and the institutions were guaranteed by the mortgage banks, in the freely traded 'mortgage-backed securities' in the U.S.

The mortgages were clubbed as the collateralized debt obligations (CDOs) by the institutions other than mortgage banks. The CDOs were protected under the derivative contracts, by the companies and the institutions like AIG and others.

Actually the mortgages (loans), given by the mortgage banks, were sold to another agency that clubbed the loans into the collateralized debt obligations and entered into the derivative contracts with companies like AIG to protect the debt obligations. They were further sold and re-sold in the derivative markets, mainly in the U.S. and Europe.

The sub-prime mortgages, the mortgages without the guarantee or any financial backing and the mortgages with poor credit worthiness were very popular among the mortgage banks. Such mortgages ensured more commission for the banks because they were prone to the failure risks and higher interests were charged for them.

The mass production of the sub-prime mortgage (or large scale sub-prime lending) was started in the mid of the first decade of the 21st century. They were sold in the finance-market using sales technique of predatory lending boarding on the fraud. The values of the securities were insured against any future risk through the credit default swaps.

The credit securities like credit default swaps (CDSs) were insured by the agencies such as AIG, once the largest company in the World. The credit securities were given the best rating by the rating agencies. The investors in these securities paid the handsome amount to the rating agencies for their jobs of giving "triple A" rate to these securities. Such falsely high rated financial instruments were exported to the whole of the World through the derivative markets.

The preferential and the sub-prime mortgages clubbed into the collateralized debt obligations (CDOs) with high ratings, given by the rating agencies and getting exported them to the whole of the World brilliantly continued to function as long as the prices of the real estate continued to rise.

The objective of the sub-prime mortgages was a socialistic and was in the favour of the poor people who did not have houses in the developed U.S. society, in the 21st century. It was based on the principle-"the house ownership is not the privilege of a few but the promises to many."

To realize such an objective and to provide the home to the homeless people, the mortgages were disbursed at the low and variable interest rates, without any financial backing.

The most of the investors who invested in the real estate which they relied as a secure investment were the losers during the crash of the dot-com-bubble by the close of the 20th century. The financial market was shadowy because of the de-regulation, the securitization and the derivatives, with underlying falsely high rated securities.

The restrictions in the trading of the derivatives and the credit default swaps were removed in 2000. The commercial and investment banking were no longer separate after 1999 with the repeal of the 'Glass-Stiegal Act 1999'. It was an important milestone in the process of the liberalization of the financial markets in the U.S.

In the 21st century the basic problem of the global economy was the economic stagnation, over-production, over-accumulation of the capital and the crisis of the work society along with the high degree of unemployment. These problems remained suppressed till the financial market continued to give benefits to the select a few in the World.

Meanwhile, when the prices of the houses were increasing and lending from the banks was at the peak, the low interest rate of the lending was dramatically increased whether because of the U.S. monetary policy or because of any thing else.

The result of the increase in the interest rate was the beginning of the foreclosure of the houses. Further, more and more foreclosure carried out. It exerted greater pressure on the home prices which collapsed and the real "tsunami" occurred not only in the financial economy but in the real economy also in the U.S. first and elsewhere later.

Very soon, it was acknowledged that the derivatives held by some of the World's the largest investment banks, from the Bear Stearns to the Lehman Brothers, were worthless. The financial instruments of the derivative market reduced into the rubbish which could not be sold or re-sold again.

The several financial institutions ended up and the credit crunch appeared. The banks stopped lending and the people started hoarding money in the houses. The credit from banks to the private individuals and to the real economy reduced. The financial crisis led to the collapse of the real economy and the bursting of the real-estate-bubble.

According to a housing predictor, 3 million households are likely to lose their own houses because of their inability to pay the instalments of loan taken for the houses by 2009. The bubbles in the construction industry were booming in U.K., Spain and parts of Europe as well and got burst almost at the same time.

The borrowed money was not only used in the construction industry but was used in the purchasing of the consumer goods also. In this way, several billion dollars were used in and supplied to the domestic markets which helped the 'global economic deficit cycle going on'.

Before the boom crashed, the huge profit expected or realized from the speculation maintained the high consumption level in the U.S. society which was based on the earnings and the credit both. The U.S. consumption spending was 70 percent of the gross national income in the beginning of the 21st century.

The U.S. economy was steering the global economy by purchasing the exports from the countries like China, Japan or Germany. These countries were giving loans to the U.S. through purchasing of the bonds and the Government securities too.

The U.S. was being indebted gradually. The U.S. people and the Government both were expanding their indebtedness. The global economy was deficit driven as the gross root sale and purchase was at very low level. Thus, the 'global-deficit-driven-economic-cycle' came to the standstill due to the collapse of the real-estate-bubble.

The global economic cycle can't be set in motion as it is based on the high indebtedness unless the sufficient amount of the deficit is not paid, the savings are not encouraged, the real economy is not brought in the front, the industrial and the productive economy is not stimulated and the employment avenues are not created in the World.

As on, March 31, 2008, the debt in the U.S. was at 350 percent of its annual total economic output whereas it was only 270 percent of the gross annual income in 1933, at the time of the 'great depression' of 1929.

The credit based deficit spending of the Americans delayed the collapse of the global economy and kept the economies of Europe and East-Asia above water for some time. They succumbed in the time of the financial crisis as they were based on the exports to the U.S.

After the neo-liberal reforms and coming up of the newly industrialized East and South-East Asian nations the capital earned in the real economy streamed into the capital market and the financial sector to realize higher profits. During last quarter of the 20th century substantial capital went into the financial market. Later on, the middle class also invested its savings in the financial sector after the popularization of stock-market speculations in 1990s.

Thus, the profits earned from the real economy did not go into the real economy. It went into the non-producing financial sector which did not generate the employments as much as required for the people. It did not help much in increasing the purchasing power of the masses to purchase the industrially produced commodities and the services.

Leverage

Leverage is a realization of the profit which means the 'degree of the indebtedness' with which market actors operate. The wide spread leverage was based on the expansive monetary policy which promoted the debt overload of the private households also and led to the excessive reliance on the foreign capital.

The indebtedness assumed absurd dimension, for instance, Fannie Mae and Freddie Mac, the largest and the most important mortgage financers of the World had the internal capital in the real estate market of the quantum of US$ 852 billion at the end of 2007 whereas the debts, guarantees and other obligations for the both of them had US$ 5.3 trillion. It was in the proportion to 1:6.5. The all round escalating indebtedness had kept the late-capitalist system de-generating.

Mitsubishi UFI Asset Management Group had analyzed that the real economy producing the goods and the services amounted to US$ 48.1 trillion globally but the global financial economy which included the stocks, the securities, the derivatives and the deposits was US$ 151.8 trillion. The financial economy was swollen up to the three times of the size of the real economy. The great depression of 1929 was relatively smaller in comparison to what we have today.

In the 21st century, the global economy is passing through the birth-pangs of the structural changes. Now the major players in the global economy are the U.S., Europe, Japan, China, South Asian Nations, India, Russia and Brazil. Thus, the World has become multi-nodal. The growth of the World was driven by the U.S. consumption in the 20th century. But now the global economy has become multi-nodal and growth has become diversified and would take place around the different nodes which would pull the global economy together in the 21st century.

In the era of the free trade and the open market, the real economy is gripped into the monopoly of the multi-national corporations. Manufacturing in the World is under the control of the multi-national corporations. The finance for the real economy comes from the banks and the capital market. From the banks it comes in the form of credit and from capital markets it comes through shares, debentures and other financial instruments.

In the time of the crisis, the capital formation for the real economy is hampered as the banks are unable to give loans to the industries and the private entrepreneurs due to the panic created by the defaults of the borrowers.

The reduced capital has compelled the curtailment of the production in the industries. The industrialists are bound to lay-off workers because of the less production in the industries. The requirement of the raw materials and other essentials in the industries has been reduced.

The suppliers of the raw materials and other in-puts in the industry have also reduced their production. Thus, a chain reaction and vicious circle, created by the less production and the laying off the workers have begun. In the classical economics it is known as the 'multiplier effect.'

The sale of the manufactured goods is reduced and the industries are not generating enough revenue to payback the loans to the banks and other financial institutions from where they have borrowed. Thus, the business of banks goes bankrupt as the assets of the banks have become non-performing.

Further lending of the banks to the industries has been reduced and the stock-markets are down. Therefore, the common people are not willing in the investment in the stock-market. It further reduces the capital formation for the industries. At the same time, the depositors have withdrawn their money from the banks and unwilling to deposit again. Thus, the banks are left to be collapsed.

The financial crisis has heavily damaged the real economy. The crisis in the economy has destructed the demand by means of the reduced purchasing power in the masses. The purchasing power of the masses has capacity to re-start global economic cycle again. Now the shift of focus from the supply side to the demand side is urgently needed to re-start the global economic cycle.

Severity of the crisis is much more in the manufacturing. In the U.S. the assembly of the cars in January 2009 was just 60 percent of that of January 2008. In Germany the machine tool orders were 40 percent less in December 2008 in comparison to December 2007.

The export based industries have suffered much more. The industries are collapsing in the U.S. Europe, Brazil, Malaysia, Taiwan, South Korea, Turkey and in so many countries. Half of the 9000 toy exporters of China have gone burst. Thousands of factories of South China are being abandoned and in January 2009, millions of workers went home to the countryside. The financial system has been bailed-out but the industries have been overlooked which is still a big employer.

Drying up of the trade finance has been one of the causes of the crisis. The underlying causes of the crisis are fall of the demand not only of the manufactured goods but of everything.

The global economy is a panoramic web of the diverse strands like the real and the financial economies. The diverse strands of different economies are inter-connected and inter-woven. The problem in one strand affects whole of the web.

The financial system, after being the first affected, has crippled the economic systems of the World as a whole. The crisis has got different meanings for the different economies of the World.

For the Western economies, crisis means the falling demand of the goods and services and that of the real estate prices. The banks are being collapsed and the businesses are failing with rising unemployment and so on.

For the African economies, the crisis has compelled the children to come out of the schools, the clinics to run out of the drugs and the medicines and the people to suffer from the hunger, malnutrition and the death etc.

In other developing nations, the crisis has brought both types of the problems, i.e., the problem of the Western Economies as well as that of the African Economies. Because in the developing countries of Latin America and Asia the characteristic features of the developed as well as of the African economies are found.

The crisis has been created by the human beings and has acquired a global shape. It could be resolved by the global concern and with concerted efforts of the people of the World.

The economic crisis in Western economies was revealed by the systemic financial meltdown and the uncontrolled demand destruction in a continual negative feedback loop. The contraction of the demand, mainly in the U.S. had affected the export oriented economies.

The primary cause of the demand destruction in the U.S. was the unavailability of the loan after the crisis as well as fewer savings or almost no savings by the common people. In the American society purchasing power largely depended on the credit. The loss of credit was the loss of the purchasing power and the demand which greatly affected the Americans and the global economy.

The Western Economy responded the crisis by the monetary policy incentives and the bails-out. The interest rates were lowered which are going towards zero. The liquidity of the money was being increased by the Central Bank but swifter and stronger recovery seems for away.

The European Union Summit in Brussels on March 1, 2009 decided that there would be no European Union bail-out for the struggling economies of the Eastern Europe. It was an economic iron curtain that separated older and larger economies of the Western Europe from the poor and new economies of the Eastern Europe. The crisis has made the single market of Europe swept away. The fault line, within 27nation-member European Union, has been accentuated by the crisis.

Robert B. Zoellick, the President of the World Bank said, "We need investment in safety nets, infra-structure and small and medium-size companies to create jobs and to avoid social and political unrest."

The impact of the crisis varies widely from one country to another. The Central European countries like Poland, Hungry, and Czech Republic etc. are being devastated because of the diminishing exports to the Western Europe and are suffering from severe credit crunch. Major European banks are facing severe losses in the American mortgages and mortgage-backed securities.

The historical evidences have supported that during the 'long depression' (1873-96) the industrialized nations had expanded their markets in the poor regions of the World as a mechanism to recover from the depression. The real strength in the global economy would come from the poorest and the remotest nation of the World as they would infuse life in the global economy through purchasing of the industrially made goods.

The economic development had begun in Africa during the late 20th century and had got accelerated before onset of the crisis. In the African economy there was a rise in the per capita income, an expansion of economies in many countries supplemented by the aid and the debt relief, a boost in the welfare spending and infra-structural development, an increase in the enrolment in the schools by 6 times of the rate of 1990s and the reduction in the extreme poverty etc.

The economic crisis and the meltdown of the global economy have retarded the very process of the development in Africa. During 2009, IMF has forecasted growth above 3 percent but the situation could become worse as the credit crunch has led to the drying up of the trade finance and other capital flows.

The worsening of the global economy means that the Africans working outside Africa, basically in the developed world would be unable to send remittances to their homelands because of the less earnings and the lay-off.

The rising pressure against the social spending would reduce the development of the social infra-structure. In such an emerging circumstance the quality of life of the Africans would be deteriorating.

In Africa, the current account deficit is widening and the fiscal position deteriorating fast. The budget was the 2 percent surplus in 2008 and is likely to become the 4 percent deficit in 2009.

From an estimate, the economies of the poorest countries of the World need some US$ 100 billion to cope with the impacts of the shocks of the global economic crisis.

The IMF said, "Now is the time for development partners to honour even scale up aid commitments....current financing constraints make it even more important for donors to ensure that aid is predictable, transparent and aligned with the policy priority of the recipients. Aid would be particularly useful now,'' in a paper on the impact of the crisis on Africa.

Some of the European countries like France and Ireland are talking about cutting aid-budget and others are temptating to follow them. The poor countries don't have resources to administer a fiscal stimulus of the order of 5 percent of the GDP boost as delivered in the U.S.

In the poor countries the increased aid and debt relief would prevent the schools from closing and prevent the children from coming out of the schools. It would prevent the mothers from dying of the birth-pangs and would save of the infants from the starvation and malnutrition.

Kelvin Watkins, the chief economist of UNESCO puts it, "Africa desperately needs a massive injection of aid and support to stave of reversals in human development. Unfortunately, the entire region is getting a massive injection of advices about virtues of budgetary prudence and some small change from IMF and World Bank emergency response fund".

In wake of the economic crisis, what could be done for Africa is that the debt could be extended to the poor African countries with supportive spirit and generosity.

The policy conditions 'in lieu of' the credit and the debt relief from the western world is one of the hurdles in the development of Africa. To get the relaxation in the policy conditions of the borrowing, the reforms in the IMF and the World Bank is required.

The lending processes of the international financial institution need review as there is a need to make the lending process fair and open especially in reference to the poor nations. The western world and the international financial institutions impose harsh and absurd pre-conditions against granting the loans.

The quantum of other assistances could be increased 'in lieu of' the debt relief for these nations because the debt creates the moral hazards, i.e. an incentive for the poor countries to repeat the past mistake.

The borrowings from the IMF and the World Bank could be made easy. The IMF is boosting money supply through the increase in the Special Drawing Rights but there is a fixed quota for each economy for lending from the IMF.

Under the IMF rules, the money supply through the SDR

is not going to help the poor countries because poorer the country smaller the allocation of SDR. Therefore, to help the poor countries quantitative easing in the rules of the IMF, like relaxation in allocation of the SDR could be brought into action.

The World Bank could do more for the poor countries in the time of the crisis, by the 'front loading ultra-cheap loans', through its soft loan facility and the International Development Agency.

The World could exert the pressure, moral as well as political, on the rich countries to keep their pledges against the poor countries of the World.

In the time of the crisis in early years of the 21st century, the Latin American economies, except the Mexican one, were decelerating with positive capital flows. The macro-economic conditions were changing due to the negative external shocks generated by the crisis. To prevent the deep economic contraction in the economies, in case of reduction in the capital flow during the crisis, multi-lateral financing was required.

The crisis in the Latin American economies is being felt in terms of the contracting export volume, the falling export prices and the reduction in the income from the remittances. The private investments and the consumption are growing but at slower rate in 2009-'10 in comparison to the financial year 2007-'08.

Thus, the consumer and the business confidence have been reduced. The economic activities are decelerating fast, evident by slashing of output and employees in the Brazilian aircraft company, Embrear, the 4th largest company in the World. In 2009, it has announced the 20 percent cut in work-force, i.e. relieving about 4200 people. In December 2008, Vale, the World's the biggest iron-ore producer has entrenched 1300 workers. In Mexico, the industrial production experienced the largest drop, due to the reduction in mainly the automobile-exports to the U.S. The industrial production contracted in Chile, Columbia and other nations also.

The demand has been reduced in general and everywhere. The economic development and the trade of the Latin American and the Caribbean nations depend mainly on the U.S. and China. The U.S. has affected almost every nation in the World but China has affected the Latin American nations even more than the Asian ones.

The growth might be negative in Mexico in 2009-10 as the economy depend more on the U.S. and that is highly suffering from the crisis. Reduction in the consumer credit is affecting the Mexican economy also. Along with Mexico, Argentina, Ecuador, Bolivia and Venezuela may also have negative growth rate.

The moderate positive growth rate might be in Brazil, Chile and Columbia. The new oil discoveries in August and September 2009 in Brazil may change economic landscape, in the time of the crisis. Some thing around 4 percent growth rates is expected in Peru and Panama in 2009-10.

The on-going crisis is different from the earlier crises of Latin America as the investors are not withdrawing their capital from the local capital market, i.e. the capital is not flying out which was in the earlier crises. The capital investment is to be assured by the big economies and the multi-lateral and the international financial and non-financial institutions, in the developing countries by changing the lending policies in favour of the poor.

Doubling of the foreign aids has been approved in the developed nations and that should be embodied in the stimulus packages for the developing world.

Asia is a big continent having economies with varying degree of strength. It has all types of economies, the small and the big, the developed and the under-developed, the developing and the emerging.

The newly industrialized economies of East-Asia developed in 1980s but the two high populous countries, China and India, emerged on the world economic map only in the 21st century with high growth rate.

After the emergence of the Asian economies along the Pacific coast, a strong trade system developed between the nations of either side of the Pacific Ocean. On the other side of the Pacific Ocean are the nations like Canada and the U.S. The Pacific Ocean trade flourished during the last quarter of the 20th century and grew up to the beginning of the crisis 2008.

The growth of the trade among the nations of either side of the Pacific Ocean has for out-stripped the global out-put growth. The rapid growth of such an international trade has given rise to the imbalances in the world trade. The Asian nations, especially China, have the trade surplus with the U.S.

In 2007, it seemed that the Asian economies were not integrated with the West and would continue to grow at higher rates due to the strong intra-regional demand. In 2008, Asian economies did not maintain higher growth rate depending on an intra-regional demand as the Asian economies were well inter-woven with the West where the Asian exports used to go. The crisis of the demand in the West destructed the supply from the East.

The contraction in the Japanese economy occurred in late 2008 because of the diminished trade with the West. The economy of export-reliant South Korea is likely to contract by 2 percent in 2009-10. The pressure is for protecting the key sectors of the domestic economy. The Taiwanese economy like that of the South Korean one is more affected by the decreasing trade with the West.

The Indonesian economy is comparatively less affected by the crisis due to its insulation from the global economy. It is more integrated with the neighbourhood economies like that of Thailand etc.

The resource rich Australia is expected to grow by 0.9 percent in 2009-10 down from 2.8 percent in the previous year. The export is the main sufferer in the crisis of the credit and the demand.

Meeting of the G-20, a group of big 20 economies of the World, in November, 2008 have signalled that there was a shift in the economic influence from the West to the East and the BRIC countries. The change is natural and be encouraged. The focus of the economic strength is shifting from the G-8 to the G-20 as well.

The growth in 2009-10, in the advanced and the industrialized countries, is expected in aggregate (-2 percent) and in the BRIC and other emerging nations on an average (+3.3 percent). The differential growth of the economies emphasizes the greater role of the BRIC countries in the global arena and the economy.

BRIC is an association of Brazil, Russia, India and China. The very first summit of the BRIC countries was held at Yekaterinburg, a city of Russia, on June 16, 2009. The Brazilian President Luiz Inacio Lula da Silva spoke in the summit that "it makes a major turning point in how our countries engage in a world undergoing profound changes. We will seal a commitment to help provide fresh answers to old problem and to offer bold leadership in the face of inertia and indecision."

He says, "after all, the world today faces the challenges that are of great complexity but that require urgent answer...We live amid broken paradigms and failing multilateral institutions. The current economic turmoil only compounds a growing sense of perplexity and impotence...".

He further spoke, "clearly modern society must rethink a system that is so unanimously wasteful of the earth's finite natural resources and at the same time condemns billions of people to poverty and despair...It is time to make tough choices and to face up to collective responsibilities"

The BRIC is a group of nations which has the 40 percent global population and almost 20 percent of the gross world production, in terms of the purchasing power parity. Its growth is the growth of almost half of the earth; its representation is the representation of almost half of the globe.

After the BRIC summit in Yekaterinburg, statements were issued which ranged from the food security to the reforms in the international financial institutions, for creation of more diversified international monetary system and make the World multi-polar, more democratic and just.

The important issues, taken into account in the statement, declared on 16th June, 2009, are:

1. Reformation of the global financial institutions in the light of the economic changes taking place in the World.
2. More or less the direct attack was made on the Western dominance in the BrettonWoods Institutions like the IMF, the World Bank etc.
3. The emerging and the developing economies must have greater say and the representation in the BrettonWoods institutions.
4. The heads and the leaders of the global institutions should be appointed through the open, the transparent and the merit-based selection process. Veiled attack was made on the dollar's role as the principal international reserve currency.
5. The strong need of a stable, predictable, more diversified international monetary system was felt.
6. The policy of protectionism, followed by the first world during the time of the crisis, was opposed.
7. Need of co-operation in the field of the energy was felt.
8. A separate declaration was made regarding the food security.
9. The terrorism, in all its form and manifestation, was condemned.
10. The comprehensive reform of the U.N. was discussed elaborately.
11. The BRIC reiterated—"the importance we attach to the status of India and Brazil in international affairs, understand and support their aspiration to play greater role in the U.N.".
12. Russian President Medvedev said, "BRIC nations want to have fair world order and ensure the safety and security of our countries and people".

13. The all decisions, important for the international community- the economic, the security and the political- should be taken on fairer basis.

Despite the indications of respite in the economic slow down in 2010 a new report of the International Labour Organization issued on August 11, 2010 has commented on the situation of the youth employment, "World economic crisis has spurred a record increase in youth unemployment". The report has stated that out of some 620 million economically active youth aged 15 to 24 years 81 million were unemployed at the end of 2009. It was 13 percent and the trend of the increasing unemployment is continued to increase in 2010.

The youth are more vulnerable to underemployment and poverty in the developing economies, where most of the youth live. The youth unemployment increased by 1.1 million in 2007-08 and by 6.7 million in 2008-09, at the global level. The annual increase of the unemployment in 2008-'9 has reversed the pre-crisis trend of the declining youth unemployment rates since 2002.

The regional trend of the unemployment as revealed by the report is that it increased by 4.6 percent in developed economies and the E.U. between 2008 and 2009 and by 3.5 percent in Central and South-Eastern Europe (non-E.U.) and CIS. The youth unemployment rate of 17.7 percent in developed economies and E.U. in 2009 is the highest in the region. In the nations like Spain and U.K. there was an increase in inactivity among the youths which shows that the youths were so discouraged that they gave up job search. The youth unemployment numbers and rates are expected to decline only by 2011.

Women are differentially affected by the crisis over the globe. The working women in Asia and Africa, who are concentrated in the labour intensive export-oriented industries, are going to be affected the most severely in comparison to those in other parts of the World. The export is highly damaged in the crisis and so is the job of the women.

Male workers are distributed in every section or type of economic activities but the women workers are concentrated in the lower level of the production system mainly in Asia and Africa. The women workers are mostly the casual, the temporary, the sub-contracted and the informal labourers. Their working conditions are the poor and the insecure. Their wages are the low and they are the least likely to be protected by the social security system including the insurance and so on.

In the emerging and the developing economies women are the first to lose their jobs due to the shrinking of the global demand of the goods produced by them. There is a destruction of the global demand for clothes, textiles, electronics and related business and services like hotel or restaurants where women are the mostly engaged.

By contrast, in the developed economies of the West the first losers were highly paid employees of white collar jobs, mostly in the finance sector and the young male workers were hard hit than the female young workers. The increase in male youth unemployment rate between 2007 and 2009 was 6.8 percent in comparison to 3.9 percent for young women.

The experience of the Asian crisis reveals the fact that in 1997 in Thailand the proportion of the women in respect to the total laid-off employees from the garment sector was 95 percent and in the toys sector it was 88 percent. In Korea, 86 percent of the female workers were the losers of the job in the financial and the banking sector.

Women, through their employment, play critical role in driving economic development in the World. They lift entire family and community out of the poverty because they make expenditures on the food, clothing and healthcare of their children from their earnings especially in developing countries.

Women can be driving force in economic recovery if they are integrated in the economic and work-force development strategies. To integrate women in the strategies and to increase their economic security important steps like strengthening and expanding safety net programmes for women and children as well as creating opportunities for women in leadership of economic recovery and policy making are to be taken seriously.

The economic crisis of the 21st century has brought the role of the international institutions in focus. It is the time for the global leadership to play fair and vital role in relieving the crisis off. But the situation is diametrically opposite as the global leadership and international institutions are not doing their job properly. The small group which is running the World has become parochial. In no way it is interested in emancipation of the humanity as a whole.

The present day crisis is so severe and so wide-spread that without the concerted efforts of all the people of the World, it can't be resolved. Therefore, the need of the hour is to improve the governance, representativeness and accountability of the multi-lateral institutions.

There is a need to change the rules and the practices regarding chairs, shares, veto power and selection of heads of the IMF, the institutions of the World Bank Group and other global institutions. The international financial supervision and the regulation need changes keeping in the mind the increasing significance of Asia and BRIC countries.

In the finance market, there is a need for more co-ordination between the standard setting bodies and those in charge of the surveillance both within and between the countries. There are the two significant issues.

First issue is the readiness of the IMF and the multi-lateral banks to deal with sudden stop in the capital flow to the emerging economies. Second one is that a situation has occurred in which the low income countries have suffered from the reduction in the exports and have no access to the capital and the finance.

To avoid a major adjustment that would aggravate matters a new concessional lending facility has to be created with the less conditionality and more flexibility. It is the proposal that the IMF has rightly made.

It is not easy to reform the international financial institutions as it would not suit the hegemonic interest of the West. The global financial capital, with the backing of the advanced capitalist countries, the international financial and the trade bodies like the IMF, the World Bank and the WTO, seeks hegemony in the global economy and limits the options of other countries to pursue the path of the independent development and the growth according to their own needs, the natural endowments and the man-made cultural resources.

11

China

History of China is long, continuous and the chequered. The Chinese society evolved in the Hoang-ho river valley more than 5000 years ago. The early dynasties of China were the Hsia, the Shang or the Yin and the Chou. During the reign of the Chou dynasty the great philosophers Confucius and Lao-Tse were born.

When the process of the consolidation of the State was stopped that of the disintegration of the State began. During the Chou reign, the pretty rulers of the local areas became independent. One of the pretty rulers was the Duke of Ch'in, who drove out the Chou dynasty. Descendants of the Duke of Ch'in established the Ch'in dynasty. Probably the name China is derived from the word 'Ch'in'.

Ch'ins began their carrier in 255 B.C. India then was ruled by Ashoka, the great. The fourth emperor of Ch'ins, Wang Cheng, adopted a new name Shih Huang Ti which means 'The First Emperor' and tried to erase the traces of the previous history of China to establish him as the first emperor.

From the time of Wang Cheng, China has always had a tradition of unity. He started building 'the Great Wall' to protect the country from the foreign enemies. The Great Wall of China still survives and is one of the greatest monuments of the World.

Pt. Jawahar Lal Nehru has written in 'Glimpses of World History'- "The Wall could hardly prevent a big invasion. All it did was to stop pretty raids. It shows, however, that the Chinese wanted peace and in spite of their strength, were not lover of military glory."

The Ch'ins were followed by the Han dynasty. The great Han ruler Wu-Ti defeated Tartars who were continually raiding the North. In first and second century before Christ China was vaster and more powerful empire than that of Rome which was greater and growing greater. There was a trade between China and Rome through Parthians, the inhabitants of Persia and Mesopotamia.

Due to the war between Parthia and Rome, the Chinese trade with Rome was interrupted. Rome tried direct trade with China through sea route but it could happen only in the second century A.D. when the Roman ship came actually to China.

The Han dynasty was ended in the 3rd century A.D. but is still remembered for arrival of the Buddhism in China, the invention of printing, the introduction of census (probably in 156 A.D.) and the examination for choosing public officers.

The Tang dynasty came in the 7th century A.D. and re-united the three kingdoms, in which the empire was disintegrated after the Han. Christianity in China was brought by Nestorians, a sect declared heretic and driven away from Rome. But Islam reached before Nestorians even in the life time of the Prophet.

During the Tang dynasty paper making and development of the gunpowder took place. The Arabs learnt paper making from the Chinese. In the process of driving nomads back the Chinese empire spread into the west right up to the Caspian Sea. Tangs fell because of the heavy taxation imposed on the subjects.

The Sung dynasty was founded by Kao-tsu in 960 A.D. Wang An-Shih, a Prime Minister of Sung, in 11th century A.D. proposed some reforms like lowering of the land taxes, permission of payment in kinds, imposition of income tax on the rich, government loans to farmers to be repaid after the harvest, buying and selling of grains by government to control fluctuations of prices etc.

The institution of the local militia called Pao Chia was founded by Wang An-Shih. Unfortunately, he was far ahead of his time and his reforms lapsed except the militia which continued for more than 800 years. Sungs fell on economic ground also, as they did not take bold steps regarding the taxation.

The Sungs sought help from the kins, the Golden Tartars, to drive out Khitans, the northern barbarians. The Kins, driving out Khitans, stayed in China and drove the Sungs the south. They became the master of the north with their capital at Peking. Kin Empire and Sung dynasty was ended by the Mongols under the leadership of Chengiz, the Great Khan, who was not follower of Islam, in the 13th century A.D.

Mongol Emperor Mangu, the Great Khan, conquered Tibet. After him, Kublai became the Great Khan and concentrated in China. Therefore, the regional Mongol Governors became independent and the Mongol Empire disintegrated. Kublai Khan completed conquest of China and founded the Yuan dynasty.

In 1368 A.D., the Yuan dynasty was ended and the Mongols were driven out beyond the Great Walls. After the disintegration of the Mongol Empire the land route between China and Europe became unsafe and the trade through land route declined.

The next dynasty was 'Tai Ming' which means bright and lasted for about 300 years. It was the typical Chinese dynasty and the Chinese people had full scope to develop under them. It is remembered for the good governance, lowering of taxes, improvement in roads, waterways, canals and water reservoirs, public granaries, issuing of paper currencies, trade and exchange of commodities and so on.

At the end of the 15th century A.D. China was far ahead of Europe in the wealth and the industry and no country was comparable to China. The Portuguese ship first came to China at Canton in 1516 A.D. The Dutch came at Macao in 17th century A.D.

The Manchu, the cousin to the Kin, the Golden Tartars, of Manchuria replaced the Mings in mid-17th century A.D. By 1650 A.D. the city of Canton was captured and conquered by the Manchus, who were aggressive people and limited the foreign trade and the missionary activities.

The Manchus began the tea trade with England in 1660. Chien Lung extended empire by conquering Turkistan and occupying Tibet. In 1790 the Gurkhas of Nepal invaded Tibet but Chien Lung drove the Gurkhas out of Tibet and made Nepal vassal state of the Chinese Empire.

The Europeans continued to shout and misbehave at the door of China. The Chinese Emperor prohibited the entry of the opium but had to face a war with England called the 'Opium War' which forced China to take the opium in 1840. It was the time of the increasing English influence in China.

The Treaty of Nanking in 1842 opened the five ports namely Canton, Shanghai, Amoy, Ningpo and Foochow for the Europeans and the Americans and which were called the treaty ports. Hong Kong, at the door of Canton, was taken into the British possession. The Chinese door for Britain was opened by the Treaty of Nanking.

France and the U.S. also made commercial treaties with China but Britain took lead in the exploitation of China. Under the new treaties China had to accept the foreign trade and the Christian missionaries and the Europeans and the Americans were to be kept outside the laws and justice of China. They were to be tried by their own courts. It was called the "extra-territoriality" and was much resented in China.

In 1858, the second war between China and Britain began. France also joined the war. There was practically no fighting, the new treaties granting more privileges and opening more ports for the foreign trade were signed by all the 4 powers, i.e. England, France, the U.S. and Russia and China.

Till mid-19th century China had strong Central Government to hold the country together. Later on, the Central Government became weak but the country was held together because of the mutual jealousies among the European powers which prevented them to take too much advantage of the Chinese weaknesses.

In early years of the 20th century the wind of the reform blew in China. With the modernization of education many students went to Europe, America and Japan to study the modern sciences and the old system of literary examination for the choosing officials was abolished.

Dr. Sun Yat Sen, famous for the three principles-nationalism, democracy and social justice; had founded the 'China Revival Society' in 1896. Because of the one sided and unfair treaties with the foreigners the society attracted the youth of nation and it grew in form and function.

In 1911, the society changed its name to become the 'Kuo-Min-Tang' i.e. the 'People's National Party'. It was the centre of the Chinese revolution as the public sentiment against the monarchy and the Manchus was rising and there was a call for the Parliament as well.

The revolution broke out in October 1911, in Yangtze Valley affecting the Central and the South China. Republic was proclaimed, with its capital at Nanking and President Dr Sun Yat Sen, on New Year's Day of 1912. The Manchu dynasty disappeared from the Chinese scene on February 12, 1912.

When Yuan Shih-Kai was elected as the President of the Republic he dismissed the Parliament and dissolved Kuo-Min-Tang and tried to become the Emperor but failed and died soon. It led to the split and the revival of the Republican Government with Dr Sun as the head of the Government in the South China with Canton as the capital. When the World War First broke out, there were the two Governments in China.

China was an agrarian country with industrially developed port cities which were virtually in the foreign control. Dr Sun, a mild socialist, tried to develop the Chinese society and the economy both and sought help from the U.S. and Britain but did not get success as they were interested in the exploitation of China. Dr Sun turned to Soviet Russia in 1924 and found proper response. Dr Sun died 1925 but the Canton Government went on adding its strength with Borodin its advisor.

The Communism was growing secretly in China and the

Communist Party was founded in 1920. The united front was formed between the Nationalist and the Communist but the former expelled the latter from the administration. Under the intense military pressure the Communists began the 'Long March' from the south to the north-west.

Despite the National Government there were numerous warlords retaining independent bases throughout the country. In 1937, the Communists, under Mao Tse-tung and the Nationalists, under Chiag Kai-Shek forged a new alliance against the Japanese aggression. After the war, the alliance broke up and the civil war began. In 1949, Chiag Kai-Shek left the mainland and went to Taiwan with his army.

The Chinese People's Republic was proclaimed under the leadership of Mao Zedong (Mao Tse-tung), chairman of the ruling Communist Party in 1948. The communism, which was evolved in the industrial background, was working well in USSR and the Eastern Europe. In China, the Communism was evolved against the agrarian background.

In 1949, to sub-ordinate the self-interest the collectivization was begun with the introduction of the commune system in whole of China and the communism ideology was thoroughly implemented by the State. The communes were the small worlds in themselves, something like the ancient Indian villages, almost self-sufficient and closed systems. They were responsible for agriculture, industry, commerce, defence, education, social welfare and local Government.

To develop industries, China adopted the perspective planning like USSR with the priorities of the heavy and the basic industries and the infra-structure in it's first Plan during 1953-57. The shifting of the priority from agriculture to industry created the food shortage. Like USSR, China adopted the concept of the 'great leap forward' giving emphasis on the small scale labour intensive industries.

During the second Plan (1958-62) thousands of small manufacturing units were established in the rural areas. The basic concept of the Chinese industrialization was the 'walking on the two legs' i.e. parallel growth of the small scale industries in the rural areas and the large scale modern industries in the urban areas.

The food shortage, failure of the concept of the 'great leap forward' and withdrawal of the financial and the technical support from USSR compelled China to focus on the agriculture.

The support of USSR led to the high industrial growth up to 1960. The cash income might be low in China but there is adequate supply of food, housing, medical care and education. It is rightly said about China, "China is a poor country without the poor people."

Under the influence of the liberalization, the relaxation in the State control in agriculture was a massive success. Huge expansion of the small scale industries took place in the rural areas. The foreign trade decisions were de-centralized at the decision making level. China attained technologies for modernization from the West. In response to role of market forces competition emerged, resource allocation improved and consumer satisfaction increased.

There was a massive increase in the interaction with the world economy through trade flows and foreign direct investments. At the same time China was prudent enough in retaining control over more volatile type of international capital movement.

In 1979, China called for the 'full development by 2000.' In 21st century, it is associated more closely with the developed world in order to facilitate its own ambitious modernization goals. It is now member of the World Trade Organization.

China stands in middle, in the present crisis, as the U.S. was in 1929 during the great depression. Currently, the Chinese economy is the most dynamic one in the World. The Chinese social engineering and experimentations are based on the agriculture.

Because of the inefficiency in the small scale farming and disproportionate land holding, it is imperative for China to bring 15 million rural people to the urban areas giving them urban based employment each year. These 15 million people are the 8 percent of the total population; therefore the 8 percent economic growth rate is usually essential in China and it is attaining such growth successfully even in the time of the crisis.

The banking and the finance are the bright spots in the Chinese economy. The Chinese regulations have kept the Chinese economy including banking and finance comparatively insulated. It is expected that due to the nature and the structure of the economy, China would be among the first ones to recover from the crisis very soon.

For the swift and the stable recovery China needs boosting of the household income, building educational and healthcare system, from top to the bottom re-orientation of the business, faster and service oriented economic structure and function and protection of the innovation with promotion of the domestic consumption.

In the multi-polar world, the shared responsibility is to be shared by China in getting rid the crisis off.

12

India

Modernization in India begins with the transfer of the political power in hands of the English. The transition of India from the medieval to the modern age was not the endogenous rather it was the exogenous, under the influence of the Europeans. Modernization of the Indian Economy began, in the consonance with the Industrial Revolution in England, during the second half of 18th century.

The Indian industrialization was basically a by-product of the Industrial Revolution and was a supplement to the economic growth of England. Therefore, the Indian industrial development lacked the logic, pattern and the perspective. One of the reasons of the late beginning of the modern machine based industries in India was the unfavourable socio-economic conditions for the emergence of a capitalistic class to embark at the capitalistic industrial economic activities.

The industries in India have been interwoven with the way of life of the people, since the time immemorial. There were the village industries, urban based handicrafts and location specific industries like the iron smelting industry of Mysore before arrival of the British in India.

When England was passing through the industrialization India was experiencing the de-industrialization, what so industries it had during the 18th century. The English industrialization heavily depended on the Indian market and raw materials and the de-industrialization of India was essential for the English interest.

During the early years of the 19th century, the first power driven machine, a spinning mill, operated by the cattle power, was made in use near Calcutta. Steam engine came later to be used in the shipping and the coal mines. The major changes occurred with the arrival of the Railways in India which ran between Bombay and Thane in 1853 and opened the scope for the swift transportation and coal mines in India.

By turn of the 19th century, there were two large scale developed industries namely cotton and jute. The modest industrial beginning had been made in respect to the coal mining, iron-smelting and the railway workshop.

In early 20th century, there had been a modest beginning of the networks of roads and railways, shipping facilities, internal and external trade. The modern banking system and other facilities, for the broad-based rapid industrial development, began during the time.

The graduation of the Indian industries to the modernization was through the British entrepreneurs and interests. Plantation preceded the emergence of the modern factory in India, as the indigo, tea and coffee growers had factory to process and get produce ready for the markets. The Indian capitalists were far behind the British ones and were disinterested in the modernization of the existing industries because of the stiff competition from those of Britain.

Infra-Structure is a pre-requisite which determines the pace and pattern of the industrial evolution, development and expansion in a country. The most important infra-structures of the time were the roads and the railways. The development of the road was ignored while that of the railway was taken as a priority due to some vested interest by the British. The Indian railways were constructed in different phases.

In the first phase of the Indian railway construction (1859-69), the railways were constructed under the counter-guarantee scheme, in which 4.5 to 5.0 percent profit to the constructing company was assured by the Government. If that profit was not realized the Government was to pay. In this phase 5000 miles railway lines were laid down. The Trunk Lines connecting Bombay, Calcutta and Madras were completed. The Feeder Lines, supporting to the Trunk lines, were in the process of the completion.

During the second phase (1870-80) the counter-guarantee scheme was discontinued. The Government under took the work on its own and the gauge of railway was reduced from broad gauge,5 feet 6 inches to narrow gauge, 3 feet 3 inches, on an economic ground. During this phase 2000 miles railways were added, mostly the narrow gauge.

In the phase beginning after 1880, the railways were developed with public private partnership. The major railway-network in India was completed by 1900 and the Railway Board was set up in 1905 which took over the Railways from the Public Works Department.

There was a debate regarding utility of the construction of the railway in comparison to the irrigation facilities which was essential to feed millions of the Indians. What was to be constructed first, the railway or the irrigation? The people were starving of and the Government was busy in the construction of the railways even using the Famine Insurance Grant.

In whose interest the railways were being constructed by the Indian Government? The consequences of the railways were not supporting and favouring India as they were discouraging the national trade, traditional urban handicrafts and village industries. The railways did little for the growth of the modern industries to take place the dying industries, arts and crafts in the Indian society.

The railways encouraged the international trade, plantation, coal mining, and cotton textile and jute industries. The construction of the railways was dictated by the colonial-politico-economic interests, not by the Indian national interests.

The coal was only power resource in India during the 19th and the early 20th centuries. After the arrival of railways in India the coal mines were developed along the railways whereas in England railways connected existing coal-mines.

The coal was known to the Indians since ancient times but coal industry was not developed. In 1815, it could be established that the Indian coal was as good as that of Britain.

The first regular coal mine was opened in Raniganj in 1820. The growth of coal-mining became rapid, after starting of the jute mills in Calcutta, during 1860s and it was funded, owned and controlled by the Europeans.

The Iron and Steel industry began with the Barakar Works of the Bengal Iron Works Company which was formed in 1874 and put its work at Kulti. The Steel and the cotton industries were truly "Swadeshi" in India. The cotton had much earlier start and was a broad-based major industry at the time when blue-print of the first ever Steel plant was being considered in India.

Mr. M.R. Kulkarni has vividly described in his book 'Industrial Development' that "India's steel manufacturing owes its birth to Jamshedji Tata, for half a century the history of Tata was the history of Indian steel industry. Tata's success buried once for all many misconceptions, fostered by the British about Indian people's ability to venture into the unknown, or about the availability of capital and their readiness to risk it''.

Tata visited England in 1900, met the Secretary of State for India and talked about his plan. He emphasized on the necessity to a total change in the approach of the Government for his plan. During the time of Lord Curzon the favourable changes took place. From England Tata went to Germany and the U.S. and brought a consultancy metallurgical engineer with him.

With the help of renowned geologist P.N. Bose, iron-ore deposits were identified in Mayurbhanj district. The location of plat was finalized in a small village named Sakchi which in course of time flourished into the Steel town of Jamshedpur.

Construction of the Tata Steel Plant was started in 1908, the first iron streamed out in 1911 and the first Indian steel was manufactured in 1913. The dream of Tata was realized but he was no more to have a glimpse as he was passed away in 1904. In Tata's plant, the Americans, who were in over all charge, were at the blast furnace and the Germans, the Italians and the

Swiss else where. The management and control of the company was exclusively the Indian.

Before the World War First only three industries were well established in India, namely cotton textile, jute textile and the coal mining. Engineering industries were developing in wake of the railways. The mechanical power was also being widely applied in small workshops, flour mills etc. Gold and coal mining were developed whereas mining of manganese was started after 1900 and India was a leading exporter of manganese at that time.

Ranade, Mahadev Govind observed in 1893 that by 1875 the Indian economic situation had touched its nadir and started improvement afterwards. Rise of the modern industries was the first step in the transition of the economy from a purely agricultural to a partly manufacturing and trading one.

The Indian industrial revival was led by the cotton textile and followed by other consumer or export-oriented industries based on the foreign assistance. The metallurgical industries were absent and the chemical industries were yet to be started. There was no capital intensive industry as such. The power resources except coal were not at all developed.

Beginning of the manganese production and export, after 1905, was the major change in the industrial pattern. In terms of both, the employment and the investment, the consumer industries remained preponderant during the pre-First World War period.

During the inter-World-War period the most revolutionary development was the beginning and expansion of the hydro-electric-power generation which added a revolutionary dimension in the industrial development. The first ever hydro-electricity, generated in India, was used to electrify Kolar goldmines.

A scheme to generate power from water, utilizing monsoon water, in the Western Ghats, was designed by Jamshedji Tata. Tata Hydro-electricity Supply Company Limited was founded in 1910 and supply of the hydro-electricity was started in 1915.

Cotton industry was India's the most important and the 4th in the World after U.S., U.K. and Japan. During the inter-World-War period the expansion phase of the cotton industry was over. The era of consolidation, technical improvement and diversification of output was ushered-in. The diversification included start of power loom, beginning of hosiery and rayon-weaving industry. Regional balance was achieved during the period.

The Jute industry was the worst affected by the Great Depression of 1929. Jute importing nations like U.S., U.K., France, Germany etc. were ruined by the war as well as depression. Bengal economy, based on the jute industry, faced the unprecedented loss and could not recover forever as after the depression the World War Second broke out and thereafter India was partitioned with Independence in 1947.

The first Government steel plant, the Mysore Government's plant, the Mysore Iron and Steel works, at Bhadravati, came into being in 1923 and started steel production in 1939. The Indian Iron and Steel Company at Burnpur was launched in 1918 and the production was commenced in 1922.

The infant industries of the period were sugar, paper and Matches. The cement and glass did not qualify for the government protection, though they made great stride in the period.

The sugar industry developed in the government protection. In 1932, the Government imposed protection duty on the import of the sugar. Within a decade, it became second important industry, next to the cotton. It spanned at both the agriculture and the industry.

The paper industry owed its growth to the protection by the Government which was provided in 1925, when it used bamboo as a raw material in place of the imported wood pulp.

The match industry developed with the support of the Government. In 1922, the Government imposed heavy import duty on the matches. It gave stimulus to the emergence of the match industry in India. The industry depended on the imported wood.

The cement industry originated with the First World War and the first cement factory was set up at Porbander.

The glass industry got revived during the First World War and had been languishing in face of competition from Germany, Australia and Japan. The Second World War provided a stimulus to the industry which was concentrated in United Province and Bengal.

Engineering Industry expanded from the modest capacity in the pre-World War Second period to a wide variety of the engineering industries during and after the Second World War.

A number of 'new' light mechanical and electrical engineering industries, based on imports, came into being on the eve and in the course of the World War Second. These industries were small and did not influence the industrial structure much.

Other new industries of the time included manufacturing and assembling of the diesel engines and manufacturing of the non-ferrous metals, chemicals, drugs and pharmaceuticals.

Diesel engine was a boon to the industry, agriculture and transport. The Cooper Engineering Company and Kirloskar Brothers were the only manufacturing units before the World War Second. An allied development after the War was the manufacturing of the electric power-driven pumps.

Tata manufactured alloy and tool steel, virtually needed for the prosecution of the War. The industries spurred by the War were the metal fabrication industries like-copper, copper steel, wire and cables.

Non-ferrous metals are as vital to a wide range of the modern industries as the iron and steel to the entire economy. Aluminum was first produced in 1943 in Travancore, Cochin from imported alumina. The domestic bauxite was used in the industry later.

Foundation of the Heavy Chemicals Industry was laid in

1941 when the production of Sulphuric Acid, Synthetic Ammonia, Caustic Soda, Chlorine and Bleaching powder was begun. The chemical industry moves around the sulpher which is used in so many industries including the fertilizers.

The ammonium sulphate was the first fertilizer produced in 1938 in Mysore. In 1943, the Food grain Policy Committee recommended the setting up of fertilizer plants. Consequently, the Sindri Fertilizer Plant was established which was ready to produce in 1950.

Hindustan Aircraft Company, a private enterprise, assembled its first aircraft in 1941. India was among the early starters in the air transport. In 1953, civil aviation was nationalized and two corporations, Air India and Indian Airlines were set up.

Ship-building had made debut in 1941 when Scindhia Steam navigation company undertook construction of a dockyard at Vishakhapattanum.

Cars and Trucks were assembled in India since the pre-War years by the General Motors Limited and the Ford Motors Limited. In early 1950s, units manufacturing cylinder liners, piston rings, piston and sparking plugs emerged.

The industries, which had begun before the Second Word War and suffered set-back during the War, were the diesel engines, pumps, sewing machines and electric fans etc.

During the Second World War steel, chemicals, cement and paper industries recorded impressive growth. Jute remained depressed; sugar was erratic and generally declining. Immediate after the World War Second, the 'older' industries received set-back.

The Indian industrial structure recorded substantial progress during the inter-World-War period but mainly in consumer goods production like textile, sugar, paper etc. The only developed basic industry was the iron and steel.

The War meant heavy strain on equipments resulting in unprecedented wear and tear. Under the exigencies of the War repairs had to be put off and maintenance neglected. The industrial development during War was spurred by the inflation and scarcities, not by the long-term consideration of viability.

There were some specific features of the Indian economy which made a temporary set-back to the industry. However, partition of the country, along with Independence on August 15, 1947, into two dominions, India and Pakistan, threw every thing out of the gear. Dominion of India became 'Republic of India' with adoption and enactment of the Constitution of India on January 26, 1950.

Almost all the jute and long-staple cotton growing tracts, gypsum and rock phosphate deposits, a large market and skilled-labourers went in the side of Pakistan. The jute industry was the worst affected by the partition as India retained most of the industries with a little jute growing area.

The Indian industrialization, before the Independence, was without the foundation of the basic and the capital goods industries. The self-sufficiency in the consumer goods proved hollow due to the lack of the basic and the capital goods industries.

After Independence, the comprehensive planned development of the Indian economy and the industry began. The industrial recovery started in 1948 following the tax concession and other facilities provided by the Government of Independent India and an active State help through the setting-up of the Industrial Finance Corporation but the cotton, Jute, Steel and sugar continued to suffer the set-back.

The Nagpur Plan of the Roads of 1943 guided and shaped the road development policy in the next two decades. Its objectives were to provide main road within 5 miles and a road within 2 miles from every village in a well developed agricultural area and in non-agriculturally developed area, no village was to be away 5 miles from a road and 20 miles from a main road. The plan could not be implemented due to the shortage of the construction material, trained personnel and fund but provided insight to the planners for future.

The first large-scale manufacturing of the locos was commissioned in 1950 at Chittaranjan Locomotive works. Another unit which started production of locomotives was the Tata Engineering and Locomotive Company (Telco) at Tatanagar. During 1948-49 to 1955-56, 1400 locomotives were imported. The two indigenous factories progressed towards the capacity production with 100 percent local components.

In 1955, the Indian scientists in association with the Russian experts ushered-in almost a revolution in India's petroleum industry, when they discovered petroleum in India.

In mid-20th century, the Indian society had dual economy. By then, the modern manufacturing industries had consolidated their position in the former-purely-agrarian-society of India. Now the agricultural and the non-agricultural economic systems co-existed. Rural India retained the socio-economic system of the past but urban and semi-urban areas had broken up the traditional set-up and had advanced in almost all walks of life.

There were different types of economic systems in rural and urban India as a primary source of livelihood. The cities showed greater departure from the past and their economic activities included manufacturing, commerce and trade whereas the rural India still had a great affinity with the past when villages used to be culturally, socially and economically self contained nations in themselves without much relation with the outer world.

There was a need to organize the economic activities on the international pattern and model, in order to survive in an inter-dependent world. To acquire and maintain a position in the global economy, there was a necessity to expand the bases of the industrialization and to increase the economic growth and development. Therefore, the development of the Indian economy was designed on the pattern of the Comprehensive Developmental Plans of USSR.

Within the frame-work of the Five Year Plans, special

attention was paid to the rural development before embarking on the development of the heavy and basic industries as the bases and bedrock of the industrialization.

The cities represented pockets of modernization having the international culture with domestic practices, bringing about desired socio-economic and political goals. Objective of the leaders of the time was to modernize India as soon as possible. In bringing about required changes, to make India modern, continuity with past often stressed, despite the new policies framed within the old traditions.

The slow transformation of the Indian society, posed no immediate threat to the ancient and dynamic cultures. What posed a threat to the Indian tradition, dynamic culture and general social stability was the scarcity of financial and material resources and unequal distribution of the wealth, whatever was, not the modernization process at all.

The land reforms were introduced in the early 1950s, for the eventual elimination of the large landed estates and improvement of the impoverished landless peasants and labourers. The traditional agricultural system of India consisted of large landed estate, small land holder, tenant farmers, farm labourers and various intermediaries who collected taxes and rents from the peasants.

The local needs of the people were satisfied, within the multiple lands holding system, as long as there was enough land and people could depend on one another for the mutual support. In the mutual support system each participant had certain responsibilities and the obligations adhere to. In such a system frequently families were involved. The land owners contributed to the festive celebrations and ceremonies like marriage or anything else in the family of a tenant. It was a mechanism to resolve the contingent situations through the mutual support in rural India. Gradually, the system broken-up but virtually no institution emerged to take place the older one despite various attempts made by the Government.

In 20th century, the rural problem was aggravated by

increasing population and fragmentation of the farm land, resulting in the surplus labourers in agriculture and farming. They could not be absorbed in the urban industrial set-up. Therefore, unemployment began to rise in the agrarian society of rural India.

In the light of the problems in the agrarian society the co-operative programmes were initiated in rural India for the socio-economic welfare of the people. The community development programme, initiated in 1952, was one of the co-operative programmes, aimed to create the infra-structures for the rural development, to eliminate rural unemployment and poverty.

The community development programme was a minimally assisted, multi-purpose, self-help project for the integration of the villages in the national modernization process and efforts. The villages were presumed to be a community of the co-operating families.

Whole of India was divided into the development-blocs, covering almost 100 villages, 60-70 thousand population and 400-500 square km. areas. The concerted actions were to be taken up to expand irrigation, improved seeds and animal bread, advanced agricultural techniques, co-operative credit societies and other social concerns like health, education and non-agricultural employment. The village development officers were to be appointed. But due to inadequate financial resources and trained personnel, the dream could not be realized fully. The successful aspects were the rural credit and the village Government.

Before completion of the land reform and rural development the planers changed their focus to the industrial self-reliance. The model of the self-reliance was developed by P.C. Mahalnobis, the renowned statistician from Indian Statistical Institute, Calcutta and Pt. Jawahar Lal Nehru. It is called the Nehru-Mahalnobis Model. The model envisages industrialization of India through the heavy and capital goods industries.

In the light of the Nehru-Mahalnobis Model the Industrial Policy of 1956 divided the industries into 3 categories A, B and C. Industries of category A were 17 and to be controlled by the State. The 12 Industries of category B were to be developed by the public-private partnership. The remaining industries, under category C, were left to be developed by the private entrepreneurs.

The spectacular development after 1950 and particularly since 1960 has been in the fields of Industrial machinery, basic metals, heavy electrical equipments, heavy chemicals, fertilizers and petrochemicals. The expansion programmes were implemented in early years of the Second Plan (1955-56 to 1959-60). In the Third Plan (1960-61 to 1964-65) the emphasis was continued on the rapid industrialization with focus on investments in the capital goods and the producer goods industries.

The industrial self-reliance implies the capacity to design and fabricate machines that make machines not just ability to manufacture the end products of the consumption. The machine that makes machines is a 'mother machine' and the industry is a 'heavy industry'. Iron steel, aluminium, heavy chemicals are the basic intermediate materials used for manufacturing mother machines in the heavy industry.

The Second Plan laid the foundation of the industrial machinery industry. The emphasis continued in the Third Plan regarding machine building and acquisition of the related skills, technical know-how and designing capacity. In absence of mother machine, the indigenous availability of the intermediate materials makes only penultimate step towards the self-reliance.

The high phase of the Indian economy was the period from 1955 to 1965 when the broad-base of the Indian economy was created, largely making self-reliant industrial structure.

The programmes regarding the self-reliance in the industry were followed by those for the food production in mid 1960s when India had to compromise with investment priorities in the industry in wake of the changes taking places in India and abroad. It was the period which faced the monsoon failure in two consecutive years and severe food shortage.

The scientific researches in the plant technology in Agricultural Institute of Mexico produced and developed high yielding variety of the wheat during late 1950s and the Agricultural Institute of Manila, Philippines developed high yielding dwarf variety of the rice in early 1960s.

The new varieties of the wheat and the rice required intensive irrigation and fertilizer well in time and increased the agricultural productivity and provided food to the millions of people. In India, introduction of the new varieties of the wheat and the rice revolutionized the crop-combination and the agricultural pattern and that is why it was called the 'Green Revolution'.

For wide and extensive use of the new varieties of wheat and rice irrigation facility was to be assured. Initially the Punjab plain was chosen for the wheat as it had canals and the Bengal plain for rice which had heavy average rainfall. Fertilizer production was tried to increase but it suffered the oil shocks of 1973 and 1979 which increased the oil prices and cost of the fertilizers.

The traditional Indian agriculture with no investment got changed into the capital intensive farming in selective regions. Because of variation in the availability of capital and resources the new agricultural pattern developed into the pockets. The areal expansion of the new agricultural pattern beyond the pockets began with the arrival of the low cost pump-sets manufactured at Ahmedabad in Gujarat and Ghaziabad of U.P. which assured irrigation facility.

The less expensive irrigation techniques of the bore-wells and the pump-sets at Government subsidy facilitated the expansion of the high yielding new varieties of wheat outside Punjab which had a developed canal irrigation system and that of rice from Bengal. Gradually the other farm inputs like tractors and cultivators came into general agricultural use along with high yield variety of wheat and rice.

By 1980, India had become able to feed its people, though regional differences in the agricultural pattern had emerged, mainly due to the differential irrigation facilities. Only half of the agricultural land of India could have irrigation facility, remaining half have to be rain fed.

The Green Revolution stopped the imports of the food grain, provided employment to a substantial population in rural India and amazingly provided agricultural produce for the exports and the industrial uses.

After 1965, the general set-back to the economy occurred, including deceleration of growth in the industrial sector. The basic and capital goods sectors were the worst affected. The mass consumption goods industries were not doing too well even earlier. The growth of the manufacturing sector experienced serious set-back.

The main reason for the deceleration of the capital goods industry, after the Third Plan, was the weakening of the initial thrust towards import-substitution, due to the financial reasons which reduced the investments in the economy. Nation faced a war with Pakistan in 1965 followed by the monsoon failures in the two successive years.

The resource constraints compelled to compromise with the national priorities greatly. Nation imported equipments from the aid giving nations. From getting aid, India was to manufacture and fabricate equipments, thus broadening its industrial base but it was not acceptable to the aid giving nations.

Following the Third Plan the phenomenon of the industrial retrogation was conspicuous which continued till 1975 after then the noticeable uptrend of the revival of the industrial production was seen. Dr. Y.K. Alagh tried to show that the year 1976-77 indeed marked a turning point in the industrial stagnation of the past decade. The most of the industry groups showed improvements except leather, basic metals and alloys and industrial machinery. In general, the industrial performance improved in the post-1975 period.

The U.S. has been hostile to the Indian Development Plans. When ever India was in crises of foreign exchange or food grain, it had to face American pressure. In the foreign exchange crisis of 1958, India was first time arm-twisted and was compelled to make changes in the industrial policy, relaxing the terms and conditions for the foreign collaborations and capitals.

After 1965, India had to abandon the policy of the import-substitution when the World Bank directed for de-valuation of rupee and re-ordering of the investment priorities in 1966. Changes in industrial policy in favour of the multinational corporations and wage freeze in 1974 were the result of the conditionality of the IMF loans after the first oil shock in 1973.

The IMF conditionality of 1980 compelled India to de-link public sector from the budgetary support, liberalize imports and foreign collaborations. India finally succumbed to the external pressure in 1991 and made the structural changes in its economy allowing the foreign capital, the collaborations and the privatization which could not last longer and India had to retract in 1993 from the excessive privatization. The private sector has been very important in the Indian economy as it is a mixed economy ever since the independence.

From 1960, till the liberalization and privatization in 1991, India faced four times foreign exchange crises in 1966, 1974, 1980 and 1991 and each time it was pressurized to accommodate the foreign capital and to open its market for the Western capitalists and the multinational corporations.

After liberalization in 1991, the Government reduced its protection to the economy, de-linked budgetary deficit from automatic money creation, opened economy to the multi-national investments and accepted the membership of World Trade Organization. In 1990s, the Indian Government adopted and followed the process of the globalization more rapidly.

Thus, India moved from the independent and self-reliant development path, which was begun during 1960s, to the dependent industrialization in consonance with the liberalization and the globalization in 1990s. Such a movement of departure created a class of industrialists subservient to the foreign capital and middle class of consumers obsessed with the western culture and the consumerism.

After the lapses of almost ten years, from 1965 to 1975, revival in the Indian industry began but with the changed focus. The Sixth Five Year Plan (1980-81 to 1984-85) was the watershed in the economic development process initiated in 1950s. The basic objectives and priorities of the previous plans did not change what changed was the operational pattern.

Various problems had been evolved in the course of the industrialization like direct physical controls were stiffing the spontaneity and initiative for growth. The various controls such as industrial licensing, quota etc. were creating hindrances in the industrial development.

The regulatory apparatuses needed rigorous scrutiny. The objective conditions had undergone the significant changes. The economy had gained maturity, resilience and sophistication. The need had arisen for the rational market decisions in tune with the basic socio-economic objectives. The fiscal, financial, credit and tariff regulations needed a fresh outlook in the changed environment.

The process of the liberalization was initiated in 1970s by dismantling the regulatory mechanisms which were pulling legs of the industry and the business. The worldwide process of the de-regulation had begun after the first oil shock of 1973. Initially beginning in the U.S. the process of liberalization got momentum in early 1980s and spread over the globe.

The industrial policy statement of 1980 deciphered the importance of the efficiency and the productivity and tried to improve through optimum use of the existing capacities. It recognized higher capacities arising out of the technical improvements and the labour productivity. It paved the path for the induction of the advanced technology, setting up capacities to achieve economies of scale.

The far-reaching policies related to imports, industrial licensing, Monopolistic and Restrictive Trade Practices (Prevention) Act and Foreign Exchange Regulation Act, import and transfer of technology, computer and electronic development, admission of private entrepreneurs to the manufacturing of telecommunication equipments, pricing and distribution of industrial products and so on were followed.

The growth was achieved since the beginning of Five Year Plans in 1950s but lacked quality, cost competitiveness and modernization. It resulted in high cost low quality production structure. The scope for economies of scale was also limited and so was the improvement in the quality and extension of the range of the products.

The first phase of the industrialization ended with the exhaustion of import-substitution possibility and limited domestic market. After 1980, search for domestic and abroad markets began, making industry globally competitive, cost-effective and cost-efficient. Path of the higher growth rate was followed.

The industrial growth which was revived after 1975 got accelerated and the industrial production increased by 7.6 percent per annum compound, during 1980-81 to 1987-88 as against 4.4 percent per annum compound during 1971-72 to 1979-80. It was significantly higher than the trend growth rate of 6 percent in the earlier three decades.

The Indian industrialization before 1980 was through the creation of the broad base, largely making India self-reliant but without much regard to the cost and quality. In the decade of 1980s, there was a marked transition with growing attention to the efficiency and the productivity through the integration of the Indian economy into the global one by opening the economy to the global competition.

In this period liberal import of technology and concessional import of the capital goods began, making India dependent on other nations for its industrialization. The technology up-gradation was required mainly in engineering industries which included castings and forgings, power generation equipments, machine tools, industrial machines, electrical equipments and so on. The great potential of the industry for export needed global competitiveness that was to be brought by the technology up-gradation.

The electronic industry has acquired a significant role in the beginning of the third millennium. The life of an individual gets halted without an electronic consumer item today. The electronics have permeated into the every field of human life and activity and hold key to the modernization. They are vital to the industry, communication, data processing and strategic sector including atomic industry, defence and space.

The information system has been revolutionized through collection, processing and dissemination of data. The electronic industry is a foot-loose industry. It is not bound to a specific location. It has a small scale production system with regional dispersal, covering domestic and abroad markets.

The Indian electronic industry covers a wide range of products and technology from the entertainment electronics to the telecommunication equipments as well as industrial and professional equipments, computer, defence and space electronics. The scope of the consumer electronic industry is increasing day by day because of the large domestic middle class obsessed with the western consumerism.

Bhabha Committee Report of 1966 is an important land-mark in the development of the electronic industry in India. Transistor revolution of late 1960s produced radio receivers, T.V. sets, tape recorder and so on. The industry emerged as 'high growth' sector during 1970s. The weakness of the industry is the dominance of the consumer items.

During the Sixth Plan, T.V. receivers were the two-thirds of the consumer electronics produced in India. The production of the computers was more than the target. Technology for the manufacturing of the fibre optics was absorbed by late 1980s. The problem of electronic industry has been the swift change of technology.

By the close of 20th century, the electronic and petrochemical industries revolutionized the Indian economy and society. The petroleum feed stocks are used in deriving a wide variety of organic chemicals. The process of electrification of industry, transport, energy and services had begun during the period.

The use of the electronic voting machines in the elections of the Parliament and State Legislative Assemblies has greatly revolutionized the election system in India in 21st century. The contribution of the manufacturing in the national gross domestic product has been gone above 20 percent due to the electronic products in the first decade of the 21st century. The manufacturing and the industrial production pattern has undergone to the significant change on the arrival of the electronics.

The Indian economy in general and industry in particular passed through ups and downs during second half of the 20th century. It was performing well with focus on the electronic industry, developed in big cities like Bangalore and others where software technology-parks flourished at the dawn of the third millennium.

The Economic Crisis 2008 has not left any economy to which it has not adversely affected. The sound and stable Indian economy suffered some scares of the crisis like multi-billion losses in the business and the export orders. Tens of thousands of the jobs have been lost in key sectors like Information Technology, automobiles, manufacturing and in the export oriented firms. The domestic or foreign investment regime has been shaken up.

Before the crisis, more than 1,500 software firms were in India with employees about 5,53,000 and out of them more than 1,300 firms were in Bangalore alone. The I.T. sector has been adversely affected by the crisis. Tata Consultancy Services had asked to leave about 500 employees in February 2009. Patni Computer Systems had laid-off 400 employees.

Majority of the Indian I.T. firms derive 75 percent or more

of their revenues from the U.S. The business process outsourcing firms are believed to be less impacted than their I.T. counterparts. The processing services account for about 60 percent of the I.T. industry and the rest comes from the core services like business analysis and financial planning etc.

The industrial indications after September 2008 are gloomy. There is significant decline in the automobiles, commercial vehicles, steel textile, petrochemicals, real estate, construction, finance, retail activity and many other sectors. In general export and core industries have showed the down turn.

The major impact of the crisis is on the small exporters and importers who are facing the heavy duty problem. The mid-sized I.T. companies are facing the problems due to the slowdown in the U.S. economy. Auto-industry has sustained the major hit and the global credit rating agency, Standard and Poor has down graded Tata Motors rating for foreign market. The company has suffered 30 percent drop in sales in India in comparison to the last year. The textile giant VF-Arvind has started releasing employees.

The tourism sector has suffered and 20 to 25 percent hotels booking for the next year had been reported to be cancelled by the international tourists in 2008. In shopping malls, the reduced purchasing power of the consumers has increased the competition. After all, the purchasing power of 350 million Indians can't be glassed over by the World, though the crisis has burnt a hole in the pockets of the millions of the Indians.

In 2007, India was the 4th in the investment destination in Asia after China, Hong-Kong and Singapore. The maximum foreign direct investments were in services, telecom, housing, real estate, electrical equipment and the computers. The situation of the investment on the ground has been changed in the light of the crisis.

Bangalore, once served as the green pasture for the investors due to its operational efficiency, is losing its craze because of the poor infra-structure, traffic bottlenecks, culture of the corruption and other social factors not because of the economic crisis. There is no active single window clearance mechanism where swift business decisions could be expected. Therefore, many potential investors have moved away the abroad. Andhra Pradesh and Tamil Nadu are losing their significance as I.T. hubs due to different reasons.

The export-oriented facilities are coming up in the Special Economic Zones to boost the industry and the economy but the results are not up to the mark. The strong will, sound technology, innovative solutions and procedural reform are some of the means to get rid the crisis off.

The Dubai financial crisis December 2009 is the most severe problem this year and would affect tens of thousands of employments of the Indians who are working there.

The Indian economy sustained in the crisis because of its structure and function but its stability may shake if the purchasing power of the masses is not enhanced within time by providing employment to them. The rural poor are wondering here and there in the search of the employment, for instance, the manual workers of Bihar, seasonally work in the agricultural field of Punjab or in the tea gardens of Assam, have an unstable life. Bihar lies in the resource-rich region of India and its people could be given employment in their vicinity so as their family life could be stable and happier.

The planned economy of India showed its strength in the time of the crisis which spearheaded after August 2008, when Lehman Brothers, a company of the U.S., collapsed in September that year. It aggravated the crisis, leading to the crisis of the confidence, in the financial market and else where. The Indian economy grew at the rate of 6.7 percent in 2008-09 and in 2009-10 when the crisis was not over, its growth rate was 7.4 percent.

From the data of the Economic Survey 2008-09, the performance of the economy in preceding years and in the crisis year could be analyzed. The facts and figures of the Survey reveal that the average growth rate of the Indian economy in preceding 5 years, from 2003-04 to 2007-08 was 8.8 percent. Per capita GDP growth was 7.3 percent per annum during the same period.

During the period of Tenth Five Year Plan (2002-03 to 2006-07) the demand growth in the Indian Economy was contributed by the investment. The foreign trade made negligible contribution but the gross capital formation was higher than the consumption.

The major shift in the pattern of demand came in 2007-08, when mainly consumption drove the demand. The contribution of the consumption in the demand was 61.8 percent which included 53.8 percent private and 8 percent government consumption.

The private final consumption in 2007-08 was 8.1 percent, due to the growth in the consumption expenditure on food, beverage and tobacco, clothing, footwear and miscellaneous goods and services that neutralized decrease in the growth of consumption expenditure on furniture, furnishing, medical care, health services, transport and communication. Expenditure on food and beverage was 42.3 percent of the total private consumption expenditure in 2007-08 where as an average for preceding 3 years was 43.4 percent

The reduction of expenditure on food and beverage indicates the increase of savings by the poorer population. The per capita consumption growth in 2007-08 was 6.9 percent. In 2006-07 per capita GDP growth was 8.1 percent. The growth of GDP more than the consumption indicates savings in the economy.

During the period from 2003-04 to 2007-08 India has been better destination for the investment of the foreign capital. The foreign capital inflow was 3.1 percent of GDP in 2005-06 which grew to 9.3 percent in 2007-08. In that period India was an important hub for exporting the I.T. services.

The Indian economy felt the shocks of the crisis after August 2008 and registered the economic growth at the rate of 6.7 percent during 2008-09. The per capita GDP growth remained at 4.6 percent in the same year. Almost all the sections of the Indian economy decelerated barring a few exceptions of mining and quarrying, community, social and personal services. The slowdown in the manufacturing is attributed to the fall in the external and domestic demand. Slower growth in all use-based categories, except consumer durables, contributed to the deceleration in the industrial sector.

The level of the consumption in 2008-09 slightly decreased from 61.8 percent of 2007-08 to the level of 59.5 percent. The 53.8 percent private consumption of 2007-08 got reduced to 27 percent in 2008-09 whereas government expenditure on the consumption rose from 8 percent in 2007-08 to the level of 32.5 percent in 2008-09.

After beginning of the crisis the consumption demands marginally decreased. Share of private consumption expenditure in respect to the GDP was 55.5 percent and that of government was 11 percent in 2008-09. The per capita consumption growth declined from 6.9 percent in 2007-08 to 1.4 percent in 2008-09. The growth of per capita GDP declined from 8.1 percent in 2006-07 to 4.6 percent in 2008-09.

The major factor which badly affected the Indian economy was the unwinding of the stocks by the Foreign Institutional Investors to replenish cash balances abroad. The value of rupee declined sharply against dollar, after the beginning of crisis in October 2008.

The value of rupee stabilized after the signs of recovery and return of the Foreign Institutional Investment flows in April 2009. The value of rupee was 40.36 per dollar in March 2008 and that was 51.23 per dollar in March 2009.

The Indian Economy was affected by the drying up of the international finance and the trade credit followed by a fall in the global demand. The robust growth in export till August 2008 became negative by March 2009. The import growth also had become negative by then.

The service exports of India were less affected till

December 2008 but thereafter, they were moderated. The growth in the insurance sector registered negative and there was a sharp fall in the travel services. Software services grew moderately but by exception the high growth was registered in the financial services which was the most hit by the economic crisis elsewhere.

The impact of the crisis has been palpable in the industry and the trade sectors. It permeated in the service sector too. The Indian Economy withstood the adverse effects of the crisis and registered 6.7 percent growth, during 2008-09 and 7.4 percent growth in 2009-10.

India is still facing the perpetual problems of poverty, constraints in physical and social infra-structure, lack of education and productive employment and the low productivity in agriculture and industry, even in the third millennium.

In the Eleventh Five Year Plan (2007-12) the Central Government has undertaken initiatives for the inclusive growth and faster social sector development.

The programmes initiated in the Plan are Bharat Nirman Programme, Mid-day Meal Scheme, National Rural Health Mission, Jawahar Lal Nehru National Urban Renewable Mission and National Rural Employment Guarantee Scheme. The Central Government is supporting the social programmes of State Governments.

India showed internal strength of its economy in the time of the crisis and according to the Economic survey 2008-09 the shock absorption capacity in the Indian Economy was built by:

1. Financially sound banking system,
2. Comfortable foreign exchange reserve,
3. Within control external debt,
4. Under control inflation, and
5. Strong agricultural and rural demand.

The major positive changes in the first four factors are the least possible. Only the agricultural and rural demand is variable and has elasticity to increase. In the wake of the crisis, demand in general has got reduced slightly in the later months of 2008-09. But it is the rural demand which has saved the Indian Economy in the crisis.

The rural demand can be increased, through rural development and by increasing purchasing power of the masses in rural India. Agriculture is main occupation of rural India and gives 52 percent employment.

The data given in the Economic Survey of India 2008-09, illustrated that the contribution of agriculture and allied activities in the GDP was 17.1 percent in 2008-09 and it was 17.8 percent in 2007-08. The trend of its share in GDP is declining but it is providing employment to very large population. That is, a large population is contributing less in the GDP.

The internal distribution of the agriculture and the allied activities shows that the agriculture and animal husbandry contributed 16.3 percent, forestry and logging 0.7 percent and fishing 0.8 percent in the total of 17.8 percent 2007-08. In 2006-07 animal husbandry contributed more and its share was 31.7 percent of the agriculture and allied activities, which was 5.26 percent of the GDP of the nation.

The share of the agriculture and allied activities in GDP was 17.1 percent whereas the share of that in the employment was 52 percent in 2008-09. It implies that 52 percent of the work force produces just 17.1 percent GDP which is an alarming situation. In a normal situation 52 percent work force should produce 52 percent of the GDP. Therefore, almost 35 percent workforce is extra in the agricultural sector and suffering from the under employment.

There is an urgent need to give jobs to the extra people who are under-employed in the agriculture. The non-agricultural jobs are to be given in the rural areas, in the towns and in the small cities, for which very high economic growth is required and single digit growth rate would not be sufficient to give employment to such a large population.

The big cities are still over-crowded and over-burdened.

The poor city-dwellers are bound to lead an unhygienic life with little civic amenities and lack of sanitation facilities in the urban areas. The problems of the urban India are different from that of the rural India.

The quality of life of the urban poor is not better than that of the rural poor. The problems of the food, lodging and sanitation are grave in the cities where the poor are bound to live in slums or slum-like environment, in absence of social infra-structure and civic amenities.

In the urban areas, the unskilled and semi-skilled people are employed in an unorganized sector mostly, having almost no social security but with much of the uncertainty in their life. They require food, other essential commodities and the shelter within their buying capacity, in a hygienic environment.

The agrarian people need high returns from their agricultural produce. The growth in agriculture in 2008-09 was 1.6 percent which was 4.9 percent in 2007-08. The reduction in agricultural growth is likely to affect adversely the rural demand which may cause low growth in the Indian economy.

The future of the Indian economy depends much on the agriculture and rural India as it has the potential for high and sustainable demand generation which needs special attention, in tune of the Western bail-outs that is given to the finance sector in the U.S. It is the agriculture and rural India which has potential to drive the economy in the time of the crisis, which is not yet over.

To give full employment to the 35 percent work-force, outside the agriculture, should be the prime concern, of the policy makers, in the wake of the crisis. It should be done immediately at war-footing. The major hurdle in doing so is the lack of the infra-structure required for the creation of the non-agrarian jobs, to be given to the people, at the national level.

The most significant infrastructures are the small and medium irrigation facilities, the small and medium power projects, developed road and railway networks. Irrigation facilities are to be developed in the rain fed areas where rainfall is less and have potential to increase the agricultural productivity. Power shortage is being felt every where in India and installation of the small and medium power projects need the special attention.

Hindrances in fast mobility of man and material are the other handicaps in the development of India. Upgradation of railway is much needed. First and foremost long route trains need speed-increase which would reduce the travel time and frequency of the trains could be increased. The speed of the trains connecting the metro cities and that of the long route trains need immediate doubling of the speed.

In 21st century the average speed of the trains must be more than 150 km./hour. The high speed trains would increase the internal and the external trade and provide fast mobility to the man and material which eventually would boost the economy.

The roads, as a complementary to the system of railways, would create webs and networks around the big cities expanding hinterland of the trade areas. It would relieve of the residential pressure of the cities as the fast mobility would induce people to live in the outer fringe in comparatively better environment.

Similar networks around the small cities and towns would help in their development. They would become nuclei of the economic activities and trade and business would develop in their hinterland. It is required as a pre-condition for the balanced development of the India.

The employment generation would increase purchasing power of the masses and per capita GDP, in which India stands at 126th rank. It is one of the bases of the Human Development Index, along with life-expectancy at birth and education measured by adult literacy rate and gross enrolment ratio. In the Human Development, Index India stands at 132nd rank out of 179 nations. In Gender Development Index, India is 116th out of 157 countries.

The entire human and the social development indices will follow the economic development which would come through the employment to the people. The creation of jobs is urgently needed, to save the people of India and the Indian economy both from the catastrophe brought by the crisis and other events which are happening elsewhere in the World.

India is suffering from the resource-crunch since long. The creation of jobs and infrastructure needs large sum of money. The huge amount of money may be appropriated from 'the disproportionate assets to the income' of the people of India. Money 'excess to the income' could be used for such expeditions and for welfare of the people and the nation. Accumulation of the assets more than the known sources of the income is not justified within the rules of laws of the nation.

Along with the Photo Identity Card or a peculiar number proposed to be allotted to every Indian the income, wealth and assets status of the people could be taken into consideration and chalked down which would help in the calculation of the 'disproportionate assets to the income'.

The wide gap between the rich and the poor and the poor quality of life of much of the Indians would not make India strong and self-reliant. To increase the purchasing power of the masses is the need of the hour. It has gone down the critical limit and creating problems for the rich.

The re-distribution of wealth, not of the existing wealth but of the wealth as it is currently produced, is not required for the poor but it is essential for the rich to remain rich. The re-distribution of wealth is also required to increase the income of the rich through the help of the poor having purchasing power, as they would be the potential buyers in the national and international markets.

13

Summary

Historical analysis of the structure and function of the global economy reveals that the root of the present-day economic crisis goes long back in the history of the modern economic system, which evolved on the debris of the feudal order and the land based economic system of the medieval period in Western Europe. It spearheaded with the emergence of the 'middle class' based on the non-agricultural economic activities like trade and commerce during the 'long 16th century' (1450-1640).

The maritime expeditions and the trade played central role in the acquisition of the territories of 'New World' where the Europeans made their colonies. The people of Europe found scantly inhabited land of the 'New World', consisting of continents of South and North Americas and made their settlements which relieved Europe of the increasing population pressure and provided external essential support for the socio-economic development.

The acquisition of the new territories infused extra life and zeal in the economic pattern of Europe by changing structure and function of the economy. The gold and silver of Peru and Mexico played the central role in starting up of the 'development engine' in Europe. Spain and Portugal enhanced their trade and commerce with the East and at the same time their trade with the nations of Europe also got increased. Thus, within a short time the economic behaviour and function of Europe got changed.

During the time of the Economic Revolution the triangular trade amongst Europe, Africa and Americas was well developed. The changes in the structure and function of the economy redefined the concept of the wealth. The formation of the colonial empire became new form of the wealth instead of accumulation of gold and silver as was in previous centuries.

After the Industrial Revolution, which began with the invention of the steam power by James Watt in 1765, technology contributed more to the development of Europe along with the trade and the territory which prevailed previously in the economic development.

India, at the time the Industrial Revolution, was one of the strong economies in the World. After the Battle of Plassey in 1757 India came under the rule of East India Company and became the most valuable colony for Britain and now the British-trade with India ceased to exist and what began was nothing short of the plundering by the British. Consequently, the industries flourished in Britain on the cost of the colonies.

The expansion of the Colonial Empire, with the industrial development, began in the new context where there was a need of raw materials for industries and vast markets for the industrially produced goods. The new markets were sought in Asia and Africa, through dependencies, protectorate states and special treaties. China was not under the direct English control but the English trade interests were served by the special treaties between China and England.

During the 18th and the 19th centuries, the industrialism and the imperialism developed inter-dependently till the every possible part and parcel of the land was not brought under the imperial control on the earth. In 1884, Berlin Conference divided Africa among the colonial powers. The expansion of the Colonial Empires and strengthening of the colonial hold over them were the solutions for many problems of the colonizers.

The mode of production and distribution was changed in the global economy after the Industrial Revolution and the World was dump with the mechanically-produced-industrial-goods. The over-production and the under-selling of the industrial goods resulted in the form of the depression in the economy. There was a 'long depression' which lasted from

1873 to 1896. In the time of the recession and the depression the colonial markets were expanded and the exploitation of the colonies was increased as a solution to the depression.

Till the end of the 19th century, England was the lonely political and economic power in the World. At the dawn of the 20th century the two other economic powers, the U.S. and Germany, emerged. England had a 'mini World Empire' and the U.S. had vast area of itself and the 'sphere of influence' which included South American nations.

Germany had lesser areas under its influence; hence it was struggling for the expansion of the colonies. Nothing was left to occupy, so Germany moved towards the science of geo-politics. In early years of the 20th century a British geographer Mackinder developed a geo-political theory namely the 'Heartland Theory'. The theory emphasized that control on the Eastern Europe was a way to control on the World. Germany influenced by the theory tempted to take control over the Eastern Europe.

Czarist Russia became a Communist State after the Bolshevik Revolution of 1917 and was renamed to 'Union of Soviet Socialist Republic', where the economic system came under the State control. The USSR and the nations under its influence came to be known as the 'Second World'. The industrialized world was the 'First World' and rest of the World came to be known as the 'Third World'.

The major developments of the early years of the twentieth century were the rise of the U.S. as an economic power, the emergence of USSR as a Communist State with isolation from almost rest of the World, the destruction of the European nations in the World War First and the rise of the economic nationalism in Europe and its expansion in the East.

The Great Depression of 1929 was a severe blow to the capitalist world. The causes of the Depression were many but the accumulation of the wealth in a few hands was supposed to be the functional one and at that time the world economy was being run by the loans provided by the U.S. and stoppage of that brought slump in different national economies.

The U.S. was the last to be hit by the depression but reaction of the Americans was sharp and their national morale was broken due to the unemployment, hunger and slow starvation. The confidence of people in banks and investment was shaken.

England recovered first, largely with the help of hidden resources and gold of the British Empire in general and those of India and Egypt in particular. Departure of the British currency from the gold standard on September 23, 1931 is an historic event and it was a blow to the British Empire.

The 'New Deal' of the President Roosevelt helped the recovery of the U.S. economy in 1933. When the programmes called 'New Deal' were lifted in 1937 the crisis came back, so the programmes were restarted again in 1938. The gold inflow in the U.S., deteriorating political situation in Europe and finally the World War Second brought the end of a decade long depression. After it, the Keynesian economic model was followed, first by Japan and then by other nations.

In 1940s, the American geo-political theory called "Rimland Theory" came into being emphasizing on the significance of the Rimland, consisting of Asia, Africa and a part of Europe. The U.S. economy was strong enough and needed the global market, so the U.S. advocated dismantling of the Colonial Empires. The process of de-colonization began after the World War Second and within a span of 20 years most of the nations in the World became independent.

The post-World War 'world economic order', envisaged by the U.S., was the result of the 'Atlantic Charter' signed by the U.S. President Roosevelt and the British Prime Minister Winston Churchill on a ship in the North Atlantic Ocean in August, 1941.

To play the central role in the world economic system, control over the monetary system of the World was essential for the U.S. The BrettonWoods system of the monetary policy and the exchange system of the currencies of the World paved the path for the U.S., for virtual control over the world economic system.

The U.S. currency was on the gold standard and others were floating. It functioned virtually as a global currency. The planners at BrettonWoods established the IMF and the IBRD. The IBRD is now a part of the World Bank Group. The IMF controls the monetary system of the World.

The United Nations was evolved at the debris of the 'League of Nations' in 1945 under the U.S. leadership. It was for establishing the peace and harmony in Europe and America in its early years. Later on, the coverage of the U.N. was enhanced and whole of the World was brought under its purview. It became the global body in form and feature but not in the spirit.

The European recovery programmes set up after World War Second ran through the grants-in-aid provided by the U.S. not by the loans. The dollar flowed out of the U.S. through the various aid-programmes throughout 1950s. The American aid was available to Europe and Japan to rebuild their economies.

Other nations, most of them were the colonies of the former British Empire, were also suffering from the problems nothing short of the European ones because of the hundreds of years of the colonial exploitation but they were left to be developed under the doctrine called the 'neo-imperialism' which was softer than the imperialism and distorted the 'national priorities' in the third world nations.

It was tried to 'Americanize' the nations of the East by the West within a short period of time. The Americanization was implemented through the West-reliant development instead of the self-reliant one. Such a development was the base-less, import-based raising of the consumption not the development at all. The neo-imperialism was a political instrument to control the nations and keep them under the U.S. hegemony.

By 1970, Europe and Japan recovered from the war-effects. The economic landscape of the World found three patches of the economic development namely–the U.S.,

Europe and Japan. The industrialized world having high production and productivity was facing the problem of stagnation and was in the urgent need of the markets to save the economy from any catastrophe of future.

The instruments of the geo-politics of the 1970s were the liberalization and the globalization. The financial sector of the economy was liberated from the national rules and regulations, making convenient for the global operators to operate in any market anywhere. The globalization was a process of the integration of different national markets into a single global network. It was practically done in the financial economy not in the real economy.

The influence of the multinational corporations in the real economy got increased since late 1960s. The U.S. de-industrialization, which began after 1965, enhanced the role of the multinational corporations, as the industries were to be installed in the nations where much of the products were to be sold. Gradually much of the manufacturing and services came in their hands with headquarters in the developed world. The small and medium entrepreneurs were wiped out and their jobs were taken over by their subsidiary branches.

In early 1990s, the economic crises arose in the Latin American nations due to the imprudent policies of the Governments whereas the crises arisen in the Asian nations in late 1990s were due to the imprudent private sector, short-term foreign investments and policies of the IMF and the World Bank.

By close of the 20th century, the Asian economies recovered from the crisis and the Russian economy was recovering from the crisis of 1998. The U.S. economy was passing through the dot-com-boom started in 1990s. Just after the departure of Clinton from the White House the dot-com-boom crashed and the investment by the people in gold, silver and real estate got increased.

At the dawn of the 21st century, the two highly populous countries of the World, China and India, emerged as the new economic-power centres other than the U.S., Europe, Japan and South-East Asia. The period also saw the price-rise of petroleum products and other essential commodities.

Derivative, the trading of the possibilities, emerged as the most important financial instrument. It is an old concept and re-evolved in 1970s to save the currency exchange and the interest rate fluctuations when the U.S. currency was de-linked from the gold standard.

By arrival of the 21st century the derivatives shadowed almost every financial instrument. Through the sales and re-sales of the derivatives in the global financial markets the sub-prime crisis of the U.S. was made global. The economic crisis 2008 affected every economy more or less. The developed and the industrial economies were the first ones to be affected by the crisis.

Year 2008 is a great divide in the world history. The bold and global economic decisions are required in the present situation, as the economies of the different nations are integrated in one. The global consensus and participation are required for future action plans, programmes and perspectives.

14

Epilogue

Evolving in the middle class of the Western Europe, the modern economic system acquired peculiar features during the course of its evolution and development. The middle class gradually grew in the economic strength and shadowed the upper and lower classes, which included landlords and landless labourers, by end of the 16th century. The new elites, who belonged to the middle class, monopolized the trade and commerce which became primary source of livelihood for most of the Europeans.

The modern economic system passed through four revolutionary phases, one economic revolution and three industrial revolutions, during the last five centuries. The system is conspicuous by absence of satisfaction and human considerations, as the greed and the cut-throat competition prevailed throughout the time and they are still continued. In the course of the time distribution and re-distribution of wealth and assets took place and got concentrated in a few hands, widening the gap between the rich and the poor.

By turn of the second millennium the economic system survived and the rich continued to multiply their wealth and assets through of the borrowings and the fraud in the deficit-driven-economy of the World. The economic crisis 2008 has become 'the great divide' in the world economic history because with the loss of the credit and borrowings the global economy slumped to the floor. After the crisis, the economic system is bound to be revamped ideologically, structurally, functionally and behaviourally in order to survive and to keep the people happy and prosperous.

The economic system of the World, before the economic crisis 2008, was the faded-neo-imperial, evolved on the debris of the imperialism. The imperial economic system was based on the core-periphery model, in which 'core' consisted of the industrialized economies of the West and the periphery included the non industrialized economies of the East. In due course of time the economies in the core increased in number.

In core-periphery model the peripheral nations were the markets for industrially produced goods and were sources of the raw materials as well as fields for the multiplication of the profits by investing the excess capital. The model reflects and accentuates the industrialization in the selective parts of the World, especially in the West whereas the East remains the non-industrialized and the supplier of the raw materials and the market for them. Such a relation had played very crucial role in the industrialization and prosperity of the Western World, after the industrial revolution.

After the de-colonization the role of the multinational corporations increased with the dispersal of the industries from the West to the East but the industrialist remained in the West. The profits earned from the East went in a few hands of the West and accentuated the concentration of the wealth and reduced the purchasing power of the masses in the East.

The finance market expanded and the massive short-term investment occurred in the developing countries after the liberalization. The short-term investment earned huge profits for the investors within a short time and again widened the gap between 'haves' and 'have-nots' as the rich became richer and the poor became poorer. In the neo-imperial regime the old imperial economic system did not end abruptly rather it continued and gradually faded away by beginning of the 21st century.

The masses are the bed-rock of the economy that is why Ford, the renowned American industrialist of 20th century, emphasized on "car can't buy car". It means that there must be some purchaser of a car. The economically over-extracted masses of the World can't generate the economic potential by themselves. Without improving the potential and the financial conditions of billions of the people of the World the global economy can't survive or run smoothly.

The global economic system like other systems of natural and social sciences consists of parts such as real, financial, industrialized, non-industrialized, developed, developing economies and so on. It also consists of national and regional economies as its parts.

The parts of the system are interdependent, interrelated and interconnected. Each part functions in itself according to what is expected from it and it functions in relation to other parts as well. For instance, the real economy functioning in itself produces goods and services and gets them distributed in the markets, as expected from it. It functions in relation to the financial economy such as it manages required funds from the stock-markets issuing shares, bonds and debentures as well as from the banks in the form of borrowings.

When we want to know a part of the economic system like to know the production pattern we have to know other parts like the sources of the fund such as shares, bonds and banking system etc. Thus, the parts of the economic system are not isolated and they stand in connection with others.

A change in one part of the global economic system brings about the essential changes in other parts or at least influences the functioning of other parts as all the parts are interdependent, interrelated and interconnected. For instance, the availability of funds and that of the technical know-how affect the modernization and up gradation programmes for the industries.

The global economic system is greater than mere summation of the parts which emphasizes that the whole can't be reduced to any particular part and no part can be accounted for the whole. After the liberalization the financial economy got increased many folds and was almost three times larger than the real one, around the close of the second millennium. In some cases it was equated with the economy in general but after the crisis 2008 it lost its grace and the significance of the real economy was again felt. Similarly, the developed and industrialized economies can not be equated with the global economy in general as other economies are equally important as parts of the global one.

The industrial landscape of the World is varied as there are large patches of the unindustrialized regions between the industrialized ones. The industrialization of the World is the necessity of the time, as employment to the whole of the workforce can't be provided without it. It can not be done without support and co-operation of the people of the World.

The previous attempts for industrialization were made under the concept of organic solidarity, from the era of economic revolution to the globalization. The system was divided into watertight compartments. The West was producer having industries and the East was supplier of raw material and market under core-periphery model which continued till neo-colonialism. In the globalization era the export-import oriented strategy of development was the continuation of the old colonial ideology in which the East was denied of the industrialization again.

The organic solidarity is a sociological concept, which emphasizes that oneness or solidarity in a society is due to complementarities of the parts. The East and the West have been complementary to each other in regard to the economic development during the colonial period.

What is needed is structural solidarity among the nations of the World in which each nation is to develop industrially in accordance with the natural, cultural and national endowments to create similarity in function and institutional structure. The solidarity among the nations is to be developed on the basis of structural equality. In a restricted sense when all the nations of the World become industrialized, they would be similar in function and structural solidarity would develop among them.

The nations of the third world have never been free to develop themselves according to their national priorities and need of their people. The structural solidarity is also a sociological concept and emphasizes that solidarity in a society is due to the structural similarity among the different parts.

To achieve the objective of the global industrialization, agriculture is to be given greater importance in the East where it is not only a primary source of livelihood but also is an economy as a whole. Agriculture should be developed like and along with the industries, in consonance with the natural and national endowments and the local needs of the people.

In the process of the global industrialization technology has to play major role, which is in the hands of the West and multinational corporations. They have to do for their sake, not for the poor because the increased purchasing power of the masses would directly or indirectly benefit them. The technology is the determinant of the industrial development of the World and technology transfer in poor countries is to take place in view of the creation of the job opportunities.

The strengthening of the real economy is another thing to be done for improving economic conditions of the World. The global investment is to be increased in it, making it the 'driver' of the global economy, for which the proper and full industrialization of the World is essential. It is equally important in the resolution of the problem of the unemployment which was tried to be solved as a by-product of the development. It was assumed that the development would create job opportunities but it did not do, so it needs primary concern globally.

The development is to be planned and is to take place in such a way that it creates maximum employment opportunities. The emphasis on the small and medium enterprises would be needed for the generation of the productive employment. It can't take place without the help of the people. The multinational corporations, which are controlling the entrepreneurship globally, have competed out the small and medium enterprises.

Following the analogous model of eco-system the significance of the small and medium entrepreneurship, which has elasticity to create jobs, could be illustrated. The small and medium entrepreneurs are homologous to the herbivores of the natural eco-system and have been reduced in number. Consequently, the lives of the 'carnivores' of the economic system, the big entrepreneurs, have become vulnerable. That's why the system is prone to the crises and these are erupting frequently.

To resolve the problem of unemployment the strong, self-reliant and self-dependent national economies are the must which were hitherto withheld. Integration of such economies into a global village would make the global economy sustainable, viable and strong. To save the economies of the developed world the employment opportunities are to be created, through the small and medium entrepreneurship, in the developing world as soon as possible to increase the purchasing power of the masses which would give life to them and would keep them above.

The economic relation between the rich and the poor is like a relation between a leader and a voter in democratic nations such as India or the U.S. In an economic system the poor are the ultimate buyers of the goods and services produced by the rich, in a hierarchical network of the buyers and sellers, as a leader can not be elected without a voter. The rich can not remain rich without the direct or indirect involvement of the poor.

The economic crisis 2008 is 'the great divide' and puts the end of the imperial and neo-imperial economic system which continued for more than 300 years or so. The focus and epicentre of the development is shifting towards the East, where it is much needed. The shift is signalling major geo-politico-economic changes leading to a new geo-politics in the third millennium.

The present geo-politics moves on the U.S. which is politically as well as economically the most powerful nation and is the champion of the democracy. No institution, regional or global, in the World, is unaffected by the influence of the

U.S. After demise of USSR in 1991, the World became univocal, which was bipolar earlier with the U.S. and USSR as poles. There was cold war between the two in the period before 1991and that was the time when 'Geopolitics' of the U.S. was based on anti USSR campaign.

In the early years of the 21st century, the U.S. is only super power but it has been unable to continue hold over the people as well as economy of the World. The U.S. with the western economies has entered into a deep crisis and the rest of the world is suffering from the problems originated in the U.S. It seems that the U.S. supremacy and its global leadership in the field of economy are dwindling. Virtually the World is now leaderless, as the leaders of the World don't have the global vision and they have become parochial. The global institutions have no global representation and outlook. The class of top economic leaders is interested in the maximization of their profits at any cost.

The political leaders have lost their supremacy and are unable to put a cap on the economic and business leaders. International institutions are no longer doing what is assigned to them and they have reduced to the upholders of the economic interests of a few persons of the West. In some of cases, the institutions are hindrances in the development of the third world. Thus, in the political, economic and social field the global leadership is under interrogation and the World is paying its cost.

The U.S. hegemony at present is maintained through the United Nations and the BrettonWoods Institutions which have lost their credibility. The United Nations was the result of the Second World War and was formed for the Allied Powers to reconstruct and rebuild their war-torn economies and bring peace, prosperity and safety among them. Later on, the Axis forces, the other fighting of group of the War, were brought into the ambit of the U.N. Further when Europe was rebuilt and peace and prosperity was brought back in it in 1970s, its focus was again changed and the developing world was brought under 'the U.N. preference of development programmes'.

The main functional organ of the U.N. is the Security Council, which has five permanent members namely the U.S., U.K., France, Russia and China. The members have Veto powers regarding the matters brought before the council. Implication of Veto power is that only unanimously accepted decisions are to be implemented. Its objective is to prevent the World from being divided into the two warring groups. The concept of Veto power prevented the war between members of the Security Council or any war between the parties of cold war but it added and abated the wider, deeper and larger cleavage in the World. The World got divided into the 'haves' and the 'have-nots' under the regime of the U.N. The impact of the cleavage is deeper than that of the war in the economically divided World.

Prosperity of the 'haves' primarily depend on the 'have-nots'. The 'have-nots' are the bed-rock of the prosperity of 'haves' as they are the ultimate buyers in the market and their increased purchasing power would benefit the 'haves', who are the suppliers in the market. If it is not so, why the colonialism flourished and World Wars were fought among colonizers for the colonies? Therefore, the most important people of the World are those who have nothing and are the gross-root buyers of the products of the 'haves' of industrialized world ever since the industrial revolution.

The U.N. could not save even the interests of the 'haves' not to say 'have- not', for whom it was primarily founded. It could also not save the people from the crises created by uneven distribution of the wealth and assets over the globe. The crises are manifested in many forms including the most severe crisis till now, the economic crisis 2008.

The other instruments of the U.S. hegemony are the Bretton Woods Institutions i.e. the World Bank and the IMF. The IMF like U.N. was primarily created for the reconstruction of Europe and later on, rest of the World was incorporated within it. During last 60 years the policies of the IMF could not bring prosperity outside the first world. In regard to the developing world, it is an arrogant organization, paying no attention to the gross-root problems of developing world and it is insulated from the democratic accountability.

The 'Board of Executive Directors' of the IMF consists of the members appointed by Finance Ministers of the industrialized countries. The World is not made of industrialized nations only. There are hundreds of countries more which are unrepresented in the IMF. Without representation how can their problems be taken into the account. The rich countries don't know the problems of the poor countries. It is impossible for them to realize the pain of the poverty of the poor countries, so the representation of the poor is must.

In the third millennium, the hegemony of the U.S. with the help of the U.N. and the BrettonWoods institutions can not survive longer as they are non-global in spirit and function. The human problems are multiplying day by day. The U.S., as a global leader, has become unable to solve the global human problems because it is becoming parochial and protectionist at the time when global vision is necessary.

Another change which occurred during 1990s was the disintegration of USSR in 1991. In the changed circumstances the significance of the permanent membership of the Security Council and concept of the Veto is lost, as the World is not divided into the two conflicting groups. An arrangement, where only five members run the World would not be viable because the World is of about seven billion people distributed among hundreds of nations not only in just five nations and each nation has its specific problems.

There is need of a body which could hear and heed the grievances of the people. The U.N. is virtually not performing its role and ignoring the poor. Those who favour democracy and human right like the U.S. and U.K. can't shut their eyes closed for longer. They are the champions of the democracy and very soon they would acknowledge the significance of the human voice and their role in decision making, taking into account their specific problems, regarding the people of the World.

The World and its people are not safe and the global economy is facing hindrances in the form of economic slow downs and crises. The major problem in the World is the reduced purchasing power in developed nations and low purchasing power in the third world which has destructed the demand in the global market. The low purchasing power in the third world is primarily caused by the unemployment and lack of economic development.

During last hundreds of years the production increased many fold but the purchasing power in the market did not follow the rate of the growth of the production because the rate of the employment generation was far below the pace of the production. Thus, the unemployment continued to increase and it was never taken as a serious independent problem and was tried to be solved as a by-product of the development processes.

Unemployment is a global and severe problem. No one nation or group of nations can solve the problem. It is more concerned to the rich nations whose business is more affected by the demand-destruction and low purchasing power in the market. The poor are accustomed to live in the poverty but the rich are not and they can't live in the poverty. For the rich to remain rich the poor are to be uplifted as soon as possible.

Other problems, the World is facing in the third millennium, are the highly skewed distribution of the wealth, assets and income with concentration in a few hands, greed (ness) of the corporate sector, declining low and medium entrepreneurship, speculation in the financial economy and the monopoly of the multinational corporations in the field of the real economy. These problems could not be solved easily without help of the people of the World.

The economic crisis 2008 has unveiled the weaknesses of

the economic system which is suffering from the slowdown over the globe. The recovery from the slowdown needs increased purchasing power in the masses. The economic well-being and the buying capacity of the people would be enhanced only after giving the employment to the people and that could not be achieved without involvement and the representation of all of the people including the poor ones in the global decision making bodies.

In the background of the problems like low purchasing power, unemployment, skewed distribution of wealth and assets, poor representation of the poor in the global decision making bodies, arrogant behaviour of the BrettonWoods Institutions with regard to the third world nations and alike, the world order needs a fresh global thinking with changed perspective and vintage point as the World has become the global village and it needs the 'Global Village Government'.

In the global village, national boundaries have become meaningless as far as human well-being and economic development are concerned as all the human beings are one and development of all is essential not that of a few. The national boundaries are important with regard to the administrative purposes only not for the developmental purposes. The general administration and the economic development are different things.

Therefore, for the balanced and sustainable development of the World there is a need of the Global Democratic Government based on one person one vote. Sooner or the later, the Global Democratic Government would be formed and that would usher-in new lease of life in the people with balanced regional development and would maintain smooth functioning in all walks of life including the economy with sustainability of the economic and cultural resources.

Article 21(3) of Universal Declaration of Human Rights states that "the will of the people shall be the basis of the authority of the government." In the light of this article, the Global Democratic Government is to be elected by the people of the World.

In the World having population about seven billion (700 crore), one representative per ten million (one crore) population would be a better proportion to be taken into the account for the election of the representatives for the Government. The Global Democratic Government is to be for the people, of the people and by the people.

Global Government

Idea of the Global Government is not new. Its root goes long back in the ancient Greek and Roman times when it was discussed in the context of the preservation of the peace between the nations. In 1329 A.D., Dante, a great philosopher, discussed it, in his treatise the 'Monarchia'.

The modern International Law was conceptualized on such background in 1625 A.D., after the arrival of a book 'De Jure Belli ac Pacis' (The Law of War and Peace) written by Dutch Jurist Hugo Grotius. Immanuel Kant wrote an essay titled the "Perpetual Peace: a philosophical sketch in 1795."

The U.S. was the first modern democratic federation formed in 1788. Later on, Switzerland in 1848 and Canada in 1867 were formed which were the first multi-state federations with the ethnic, cultural and lingual diversity under a common Government.

Ulysses S. Grant commented, "I believe at some future day, the nations of earth will agree on some sort of congress which will take cognizance of international questions of difficulty and whose decisions will be as binding as the decisions of the Supreme Courts are upon us".

The Inter-Parliamentary Union, organized by Cremer and Passy, consisting of the legislators from many countries in 1886, was the first embryonic World Parliament.

The attempts to develop the international institutions for peaceful resolution of the international disputes were made in the first half of the 20th century. The Hague conferences of 1899 and 1907 gave way to the League of Nations (1919-

1938) which was replaced by the U.N. formed in 1945. The U.N. adopted the Universal Declaration of Human Rights in 1948.

The formation of the effective Federal World Government was recommended by the prominent personalities like Albert Einstein, Winston Churchill, Bertrand Russel and Mahatma Gandhi et.al.

Albert Einstein has rightly stated that "There is no solution for civilization or even the human race, other than the creation of the world government."

A very popular book named the "One World" of Wendell Wilkie came in 1943. Emery Reves wrote in his book "The Anatomy of Peace" in 1945, "There is no first step to world government; the world government is the first step". He advocated for replacing the U.N. with a federal World Government. The World federalist movement in the U.S. gave birth to the World Federalist Association which later on became the Citizens for Global Solutions.

In 1948-49, UNESCO carried out the opinion polls for the World Federal Government which was favoured in the six European nations but was rejected in Australia, Mexico and the U.S. Davis announced the formation of the "World Government of World Citizens", based on one spirit, one world and one mankind on September 4, 1953.

The federal movement of 1990s succeeded in establishing the International Criminal Court in 2002. It created the European Union and enlarged the agreement of Maastricht Treaty on which the E.U. was based upon in 1992. By 2007-expansion of the E.U. there were 27 member nations with about half a billion population.

The E.U. provided an example of the continental associations and led to the formation of the African Union in 2002 and the Union of South American Nations in 2004. The African union consisting of 53-African states aimed to have a single currency and a single integrated force to secure the democracy, human rights, sustainable economy with the creation of an effective common market.

The Union of South American Nations is founded on the European Union model incorporating all the independent States of South America.

The Organization of Central American States, the Association of South-East Asian Nations and South-Asian Association of Regional Co-operation are some of the regional associations. There are multitudes of the regional associations aggregating most of the nations of the World at different stages of the evolution.

A conspiracy Theory is also prevalent about the formation of the World Government. According to it, a group of powerful and secretive persons is planning to control the World through an autonomous World Government which would replace the sovereign States.

Conspiracy to rule the World is plotted through the combinations of the World affairs related to the political, financial, social, psychological and other issues. The instruments of the conspiracy are supposed to be military industrial complexes, the council of Foreign Relations, the IMF, private bankers, the multinational corporations and others. There are about 20 functional organizations affiliated to the U.N. like the Economic and Social Council, WHO, ILO and so on. The IMF, the World Bank and the WTO are the politically more important. The conspirators might use these organizations in their interest.

The unemployment and low purchasing power of the masses have inflicted heavy damage to the economic conditions of the conspirators of the World Government. They would be in great loss in the changed situation as their economic well-being depends primarily on the poor of the World whose freedom and the sovereignty they want to confiscate in the name of the World Government.

Development of the communication and information system has made the World a complex web of the international co-ordination and influence. After emergence of the economic crisis 2008, need of the Global Democratic Government is being felt every where in the World as none is to take care of the problems arisen before us mainly in the third world.

The demand for the Global Democratic Government, after the 'great divide', the economic crisis 2008, is different from the steps taken in this regard in the previous centuries. The previous attempts were for the formation of the Federal Government that was to be a union of the different nations and that was based on one nation one vote and on this principle the U.N. is formed.

The present proposal is for the directly elected Global Democratic Government of the people which is to be based on the principle of one person one vote. The concerted-efforts of the people, in the form of the Global Democratic Government, are required for the solution to the global problems like the economic crisis 2008.

The challenges which are before the Global Democratic Government would thwart the very purpose for which it is being proposed. Therefore, the success of the government depends on facing the challenges of the general problems of insecurity, lack of trust, dwindling confidence and the greed. These are the main hurdles in the formation of the Global Democratic Government and if it is anyhow formed they would create hindrances in its running.

The feeling of insecurity is so overwhelmingly spread in the society that everyone wants to make things secure forever and it has percolated from the top to the bottom. It has encompassed almost every country, group or the individual in it. It has created panic everywhere and people are afraid of the insecurity in every walk of life.

The countries are so fearful that they are piling different types of lethal weapons and are incurring huge budget expenditures, realized from the common people bolstering their security and defending their virtual boundaries. The divide between the countries are so widely exaggerated due to the fear and insecurity, that it has dwarfed the development programmes, democratic values and human dignity.

The different groups and associations in the world are not far away from the dragon of the insecurity and they are conspiring against each other. Every time and everywhere a group attempts to humiliate and harm others for the sake of its security but it is still far away because the security perpetuates in the harmony not in disharmony. The individuals having feeling of insecurity are adopting the corrupt means to make money and to make themselves secure in the present circumstances.

The issue of the insecurity had been the backbone of the 'cold war' between the U.S. and former USSR during the later half of the twentieth century. The 'cold war' was one of the significant events of the second half of the twentieth century and the problems created by it have affected the World as it was virtually divided into the two warring groups and either of the two always tried to gobble other up.

Afghanistan, the landlocked and mountainous State, situated between the Indian Sub-Continent and the Arabian Peninsula and surrounded in north by the independents of former USSR, was one of the victims of the 'cold war'. After independence from the British Rule in 1919 it had close relations with USSR which was its reliable ally.

USSR, under the geo-political compulsion, needed an access to the Indian Ocean to eye on the petroleum rich Middle East and geo-politically turbulent South Asia. The path of former USSR to the Indian Ocean goes via Afghanistan and the presence of USSR in it was helpful in such an ambition.

After Second World War Afghan-Russia relation strengthened and Communism spread in Afghanistan. It was the time of 'cold war' and such a development was not pleasant to the U.S. The U.S. adopted all means, including the spread of hatred and the internal instability, to restrict the increasing influence of the Communism and that of USSR in Afghanistan.

The U.S., with some other nations, supported financially,

emotionally and psychologically to the 'Mujahidins' of Afghanistan during the late 1970s and the early 1980s. Some other nations of the World also supported the 'Mujahidins' with man and material. The 'Mujahidins' were the warriors who were against the presence of the Communism and USSR in their country.

When 'Mujahidin Movement' became strong in Afghanistan the Russian army came in support of Afgan-Government to crush the movement. It was an opportunity for the U.S. to humiliate USSR and to throw it out of Afghanistan. The U.S. capitalized the opportunity and intensified the action against the USSR in Afghanistan and was winner in this very 'cold war'.

Regarding the U.S. support to the 'Mujahidin Movement', Zbigniew Brzezinski, U.S. President Jimmy Carter's National Security Advisor said, "what is most important to the history of the world? The Taliban or the collapse of the Soviet empire? Some stirred-up Moslems or the liberation of Central Europe and the end of the cold war?"

The "cold war" came to an end in which the U.S. was interested and USSR got disintegrated in 1991 into the fifteen independent States. The U.S. was not interested in the welfare of the people of Afghanistan where it had sowed the seeds of the hatred and internal instability. Other supporters of the 'Mujahidin-movement' also capitalized the vulnerable condition of Afghanistan in their interests, as none was interested in the welfare of the poor hungry people of the nation whose plight is still getting intensified.

With the departure of USSR from Afghanistan, the anti-USSR sentiment of the people got changed into the anti-U.S. sentiment and a new movement emerged on the debris of the 'Mujahidin-movement' called the 'Taliban-movement'. It was against the West in general and the U.S. in particular. The U.S. suffered the Taliban attack at the Trade Tower on September 11, 2001. Presently, the U.S. is almost directly fighting with the Taliban and searching a middle path to leave Afghanistan.

There are several movements in the World which are opposing interference or the presence of the foreign powers on their land. Security is the main concern in them. The poor countries of the third world are facing hardship in saving their man and material and they are victim to the geo-politics. The prevailing poverty in such countries has left hundreds of millions of unemployed youths to choose any path of economic activity which seems them suitable. Such youths are emotionally and psychologically brainwashed and are thrown into the activities like terrorism by others. The others are capitalizing in their interest the vulnerable conditions of the poor who are suffering from the lack of security in their life.

If the feeling of security evolves among the persons who are leading life in scarcity then the supply of men to the terror activities could be reduced. The poor could be brought into the global mainstream by providing proper job opportunities now those are available for anti-social activities. The people would leave gun if they have butter, the proper means of livelihood. The gun and butter can't run together whether at individual or at the national level. At individual level, to some extent, the unemployed youths have gun and those who have proper employment are leading a peaceful life having butter.

There was a dispute over the issue of 'gun and butter' in the U.S. in the later years of 1940s. The Council of Economic Advisors was established by the Employment Act of 1946 in the U.S. to provide economic analysis and advice on the development. Its aim was to implement a wide range of domestic and international economic policy issues.

A dispute over 'gun and butter' had broken out between Chairman Nourse and member Leon Keyserling in 1949. A choice was to be made between 'gun and butter'. According to Nourse who believed that heavy expenditure on war and high standard of living of people was not manageable at a time. But he could not sustain the onslaught of Leon Keyserling who believed that an expanding economy of the U.S. could bear the large defence expenditures without sacrificing an increased standard of living. He was supported by the President Truman's advisors Dean Acheson and Clark Clifford. Nourse resigned as Chairman and warned against the dangers of having 'gun and butter' together.

The sense of the insecurity reduces the trust between nations, groups or individuals. The trust has been evaporated from the World due to the feeling of the insecurity prevalent among individuals or nations. The lack of trust is a global feature and it could be found any where in the World. In the developed world distrust is more prevalent and surfaced up during the economic 2008 when the business fell in trouble.

The trust acquired a functional role during the crisis when the business leaders wanted recovery with the help of political ones but in their opinion the business leaders were greedy and incapable of dealing with the business so they did not help them to the extent they needed, because there was lack of trust between the two. It is an example of distrust in the West. Similarly in the banking system the banks fell and falling continued during the crisis as bankers and customers didn't trust each other.

The trust is a cementing agent and bridges the gap between the nations, groups and the individuals and it gets weakened because of the short-term self interest which has become characteristic feature of the era and it is a hindrance in the path of development and social harmony. The trust is the most important element required for the formation of the Global Government which needs the people as the Government is of the people, by the people and for the people.

Therefore, there is need to build up trust in the system but what is happening in the World is something else. The distrust is getting built up by the widening inequality, corporate greed and lack of monitoring at global level. The global leaders have become protectionist at the time when globalization is to be accentuated which knowingly or unknowingly is increasing distrust. The World needs trust as an instrument of recovery from the crisis which is or may arise before us in future.

In such a society where insecurity prevails with the lack of the trust among the members of it what would the level of the confidence of the people? Naturally, the people would not have confidence in themselves and would not have trust on others. Lack of the confidence reflects in the decisions taken regarding the social, economic, political and religious activities in the society. The dwindling confidence prevents the different types of leadership from taking bold decisions regarding the formation and reformation of the society which is manifested in the slow recovery from the economic crisis.

The greed is another problem the World is facing with and which has engulfed almost every one. It functions more at individual level. It is a general perception of the people that the greed, resulted in money making, has become determinant of the human activities. The materialistic greed, the greed of pelf and power, functions as a magnet and compels individuals to follow the path of the short-term gain to fulfil their desire.

Almost none is out of the sphere of the greed; even the responsible persons are not discharging their duties properly and they are involved in the accumulation of wealth through any means, fair or foul. Every one, marred by the feeling of the insecurity, is accumulating wealth for one's adverse days in advance. None is interested in delaying or preventing the adverse days. But they are involved in the "crisis management" which will come in future.

It is widely believed that the business leaders through multinational corporations are highly interested in the making of high profits at any cost. To attain their goal they are influencing the political leadership over the globe. Similarly other leaderships like social, religious etc. have oriented themselves towards pelf and power through any means. It seems that the wealth has become 'summom-bonnum' of the life of the human beings and values, norms, sustainability and etc. have relegated to the back seat.

The problems of insecurity, trust and confidence could be overcome through the incorporation of the different groups of people into a global mainstream which is a panoramic web of diverse strands of thoughts and ideas to knit the people. It also facilitates the unification of the World into a household or in a global village which consequently paves the path for the formation of the Global Democratic Government.

The policies, like protectionism being followed by the West in the time of economic crisis, are hindrances in the formation of the global mainstream. The protection by separation and isolation is dangerous and strikes at the root of the international solidarity required for the well-being of the people residing on the earth.

The necessary theme behind the formation of the global mainstream is that the different groups having diverse socio-cultural and the economic background are integrated in a common body. Such integration is a consciously carried out phenomenon and is essential for the global planning processes required for regionally balanced economic and cultural development.

The significant question is what is the "mainstream" to which the diverse groups of the World are to be knitted?

The techno-scientific-economic development, which has occurred during last a few centuries in the West, has contributed much to the World but it has not taken place uniformly. A considerable part of the earth and a large population is still devoid of the development. To equate this proposition with the global mainstream is not only dangerous but is antithetical to the diversity of the World also. The sustainable, safe, prosperous and progressive world requires the classless harmonious society where inequality of all kinds is to be abolished and the secularism is to be practiced.

Another aspect of the global mainstream is the common productive organizations which too are essential for it and are the bases of the economy. Barring a few small patches, in most part of the World the production organizations are almost similar with varying intensity, depending on the level of the economic development. A planned global economy, with technically upgraded productive organizations over the globe, meeting with all the socio-economic challenges is indispensable for the global integration. The lop-sided development coupled with the national and the regional imbalances will slacken the very process of the global integration.

The other proposition regarding global mainstream may be formed behind the Gandhian values and ideas which are based on morality, tolerance and non-violence. For Gandhiji, the promotion to the religious neutrality would liberate the masses from their subservience to the religious hegemony. For him, secularism was the foundation of our political life making every individual a better human being in his personal life. For him, every one has to work together to make the World the happy home of a liberated and cultured people, who share one another's labour in a modernized egalitarian society.

The Gandhian ideas in the global integration and a developmental model that emerges seem viable and essential as the moral values have deteriorated in the modern World, which is an irreparable loss. It is the Gandhian values and philosophy which enlightens us in such circumstances and paves the path for the peaceful co-existence of the human beings. It advocates live and let live others which signify that the consideration of others is equally important in one's life. At present the people have less consideration for others as they are seen as the hindrances in their pleasure and happiness. Adherence to the moral values and its importance in the human life strengthens the democratic values, collectiveness and the human dignity.

A visible and significant aspect of the global mainstream is the diversity and in its terms the World has different levels, from the national to the individual. Besides the diversity of nations there are diversities of cultures, ethnic groups, religions, languages and so on. But one need not be unduly frightened about the existence of the diversity as the World is made of different nations and regions with a large variety of the cultural propositions. The World is heterogeneous, therefore integration is needed.

In the global integration, the essential principle is the unity in the diversity where (a) uniqueness of each nation is to be kept alive; (b) the nations must be healthily knitted to the global mainstream; and (c) the forces which disrupt unity need to be curbed. The concept of unity does not necessarily presume the existence of a monolithic structure. Unity always results from the existing diversities.

The World is a mosaic of the different continents and the nations with a diversity of human population. Every individual in the World is a member of a nation, region, ethnic group, religion and so on. Loyalty to each of these segments is instilled in the very process of the upbringing. These cross-cutting ties of loyalty to various segments stand in a balanced opposition to others of structural equivalence which has led some to believe that every segment or group is in minority and is in the fringe in one way or another. Cutting across all these minority statuses the global unity is the highest level of integration.

Every person is integrated at global level and at the same time he is loyal to his nation and to the different groups to which he is adhered to. It is unnatural and impossible to eliminate differential loyalties of people in the World. The highest level of loyalty-the global loyalty-expects that lower levels of loyalty exist simultaneously.

There is a perennial fear that loyalties based on nation or some thing else can always make their appearance in political terms. From the national loyalties, the nationalism or from the regional loyalties, the regionalism can precipitate. The threats to the global integration are contained in the very notion of the diversity but at the same time the unity results from the diversity. The diversity is the conspicuous feature of the World and for its sustainability we have to make it the melting pot of the diversities. Then what is the global mainstream? Do Westernism, democratic processes, productive organizations and secularism collectively make up the mainstream? Do the Gandhian values and philosophy form the mainstream?

In nut shell, it could be imagined that there is a global mainstream in which all diversities should (and must) melt. This 'taken-for-granted' concept emphasizes that it is that culture of the World where all the diversities melt, where the notion of segregation is not held and a group is united with the other transcending individual, cultural, ideational and national differences.

Undoubtedly the global mainstream consists of a set of modern values like equality, democracy, modern productive processes and secular ethics. But these values need to be translated in the context of the global reality. For instance the modern productive processes should not alienate the third world rural masses by concentrating all its gains in the developed world. For the developmental and planning processes all the nations and the groups within them like pastoralists, peasants, workers, etc. must have equal weightage. And depending upon the gravity of the problems of each nation and group, specific allocation may be made. The mainstream conceived as a cultural milieu has to result from a set of values adapted and synchronized to the global conditions.

Conclusion

In the first decade of the first century of the third millennium the economies of the different nations are interwoven into a web and an event in an economy affects the others. Nothing is the local every thing is the global. The World is united into a single unit called the global village. Instead of territories of the nations, their inhabitants have become more important in the present economic context. The political control over the territories for the economic interests has lost its significance.

The technological revolutions have united the territories of the World on one hand and on the other hand they have diversified the economic activities and the trade. The trade in the commodities, services, intellectual properties, the visible and the invisible has been metamorphosed, under the influence of the technological changes.

In the third millennium the orientation of the economy has been changed from the mass production and scale economies to the flexible production with emphasis on the innovation, innovation rents, scope economies and rapidly changing and differential pattern of the consumption.

The knowledge, ideas and technology embedded in services and manufactured products are the keys to the growth. The real economy has become the victim of the monopoly and the financial one has become the speculation-prone suffering from the risk, uncertainly and constant changes.

The global openness, inter-changes and inter-dependency have exploded the global finance in the form of the short-term capital flow which played an adverse role in the Asian crisis of late 1990s.

The financial globalization in particular and the globalization in general have greatly diminished the national economic autonomy. The practices of the production and exchange have been transformed in the developed world. There are fewer people who are involved in the agriculture and the factory in comparison to the past. The new work-force includes the intellectual persons with the changes in the nature of the work.

The global exchange system, including commodities and money, has been reframed in the light of the computer revolution, digitalization and electronic information processing techniques and technologies. Technology has become the real controller of the global economy not the trade and territory which used to be the controller in the past.

The capitalism of the third millennium might be called the electronic-techno-scientific capitalism. The adjectives of capitalism increased with the development of the Science and Technology in due course of time.

The new financial instruments like derivatives have been built upon the older processes. The derivatives are the contracts specifying rights and obligations based upon and deriving values from the underlying instruments. In the derivative market the value oriented and abstracted future possibilities are traded. The objects and services have become secondary items of exchange in the market. Monopoly is a dominant feature in the real Economy. There is a competition between the nations and the corporations for control over the resources and markets in the World.

Another significant feature of our economic system is the unequal distribution of the wealth and income which has been aided and abated by the monopoly and speculation. The World Bank Development Indicators of 2008 throw light on the unequal distribution of the wealth.

The total population of the World was 6.46 billion in 2005. Only 20 percent population (1.31 billion) was above the poverty line defined as US$ 10 per day per person (the American poverty line) at the purchasing power parity in 2005. Only 5 percent population of the third world was above this poverty line. The World's the wealthiest countries (approx. 1 billion people) accounted for 76 percent of the World GDP.

The World's billionaires, just 497 persons, accounted for over 7 percent of the World GDP. The low income countries (approx. 2.4 billion people) accounted for just 3.3 percent of the World GDP. The middle income countries (approx. 3 billion people) accounted for 20.7 percent of the World GDP.

Below the extreme poverty line, defined as US$ 1.25 per day per person, were approx. 1.4 billion people who resided mainly in the Sub-Saharan Africa, South Asia and in some other parts of Asia, rarely found else where.

Both, the well-off and extremely poor people, don't play major role in driving the global economy. The well-off have purchasing power but they are few in number in comparison to the total population of the World and can't pull the global economy alone. The extremely poor are the too poor and have very little potential to play a role in the global economy. They need intensive care and assured protection before their integration in the global economic system as an important player in the economy.

The remaining population [6.46-(1.31+1.40)] =3.75 billion falls in the bracket of the middle class. It has potential to drive the global economy but in the time of economic crisis 2008 it has lost its confidence in the market. The savings and the purchasing power of the middle class infuse strength in the economy which has evaporated during the crisis.

In the global economic system, the middle class play the most important role. For proper functioning of the world economy its financial strength is the backbone and the bed-rock both. Therefore, it is imperative for the World to infuse the purchasing power in the middle class and it could be done only by creating the opportunities for the productive employment for them. In the time of the crisis, the global attention is needed for the creation of the employment.

The most of the unemployed persons are unskilled or semi skilled poor people who have limited mobility for jobs in comparison to the skilled and highly qualified persons like computer engineer or information technology engineer who can work any where on the earth.

The scope for jobs of unskilled or semi skilled manual labourer is limited as they could be given the employment by the small and the medium entrepreneurs more easily in comparison to the big entrepreneurs and the multinational corporations whose capacity to provide employment to them is limited.

In 1999, there were 60,000 multinational corporations worldwide with 5,00,000 foreign subsidiaries, selling US$ 9.5 trillion of goods and services across the globe, accounting for at least 20 percent of the world production and 70 percent of the world trade (Held and McGraw, p. 6).

The multinational corporations are guided by the concept of the 'global laissez-faire' whereas the idea of the 'microeconomic *laissez-faire* has become obsolete. They are producing a variety of products worldwide and under taking economic activities in hundreds of countries. They are producing and manufacturing almost every item from the big to the small, the complicated to the simple, capital intensive to non-capital intensive, knowledge intensive to labour-intensive and so on.

The fall in purchasing power and the rise in unemployment are due to the monopoly in the real economy and the speculation in the financial economy. The medium entrepreneurs, who have potential to absorb the poor, have lost their significance, after being competed out by the multinational corporations. It is an unhealthy symptom in the global economy.

The multinational corporations and the big entrepreneurs have taken over the functions of the small and the medium entrepreneurs, leaving behind them unemployed who have potential to provide jobs to the poor people. Thus, a distorted pyramid of the economic system, with weaker middle section, has emerged and purchasing power of the market is reduced.

An analogy emerges between the natural eco-system and the global economic system. In an eco-system a food chain exists in which at the top is lion, a carnivore which depends on deer, rabbit or other herbivores for survival. Herbivores depend on quantum of the grasses grown in the system. The quantum of grass indirectly determines the life and number of lions, in an eco-system. Thus, to save the lion grasses are to be grown in the eco-system.

Similarly, in an economic system, the 'economic lions' of the World depend more on the upper middle class which also includes the small and the medium entrepreneurs who are directly involved in the business relations with the 'economic lions'. The small and the medium entrepreneurs depend for their business on the poor of the World, who are also the gross-root buyers of the globally produced goods and services. Thus, the survival of the economic giants depends on the poor buyers in a hierarchical system.

Thus, for the sake of the big entrepreneurs and the multinational corporations, purchasing power of the general masses is to be increased and maintained at a sustainable level so as their products could be sold in the market. In the age of the multinational corporations, the small and the medium producers and manufacturers have been competed out of the market because the multinational corporations provided good quality products at low cost.

The gain in term of the quality and cost was offset by the loss of the jobs of the small and the medium entrepreneurs and the associated poorer workers. The unemployment left them in extreme poverty and they were struggling for mere survival. In the regime of the multinational corporations the people are getting good quality products at low cost but their purchasing power is gradually getting reduced which made them denied of the basic needs of the life.

In 2009, the good quality products at low cost are not available amply in the market as with the increasing cost of the products of day to day use the manufacturer is compromising with the quality to keep the prices low. It is hard to digest for those who believed that multinational corporations produced quality items. It is true in the normal time but not in the time of the crisis.

Because of the reduced purchasing power the products are neither being sold nor the people are getting the good quality products at low cost. In this situation a vicious circle of crisis is likely to start which may bring standstill in an economy.

To overcome the situation which has occurred before us it is the need of the hour to increase the purchasing power in the masses which would result in selling of products giving strength to the economy.

Tata is a steel giant of India and produces heavy vehicles including locomotives. In the time of the crisis when purchasing power of the people is got reduced the sale of the vehicles of Tata is gone down. During past few years Tata has started production of so many things of day today use including the salt. Tata has monopolized many products including the salt which could be produced by the small and the medium entrepreneurs.

There are so many entrepreneurs like Tata in the World who are producing from the big to the small items. The small items like the salt or others could be left for the small and the medium entrepreneurs who would generate more employment among the poor mainly for unskilled ones. It would consequently increase the purchasing power in the market. The heavy vehicles of Tata would be purchased by the small and the medium entrepreneurs who would work as a bridge between the entrepreneurs like Tata and the poor masses maintaining the chain of the business.

However the question is who is going to decide that what would be produced and by whom? After the emergence of the economic crisis 2008, the scenario of the global economy has drastically changed. The increased greed of the people and corporate world has created a situation in which the credit and the trust have evaporated from the scene of the World and the institutions like the U.N. have lost their credibility and the new global institutions are urgently needed to answer such questions.

To face the global problems like the crisis the industrialized world including the U.S. is not showing the global vision and global perspective but following a parochial path of the protectionism as if the problem is outside. They are planting bushes around their nations to prevent the outsiders. The problem is not outside rather it is inside the nation and it could be resolved by the global vision and global action in association with the people of the World.

The record of the global institutions such as the IMF, the World Bank and other international institutions has not been satisfactory during the time of the Asian crisis of 1990s. They were not interested in opening the market of commodities but they were interested in the opening of the capital markets which by nature is unstable and volatile and requires the State protection.

The policies of the West in association with the international institutions have given birth to the crises like slowdown in the global economy which has affected the rich more. The poor were the poor and are still poor but the rich are becoming the poor which they were not and they are not adapt to live in the poverty. For the rich to remain rich the poor are to be uplifted.

The democracy is a form of the Governance in most of the nations, barring a few exceptions. The U.S., U.K., and others are its champions of the democracy which has resolved so many problems in the past. Answers to the questions like 'what is to be produced and by whom' is to be given by the Global Democratic Government that would be formed by the people, for the people and of the people. The problem is global and its solution is to be global. The global leadership with the global perspectives and the global vision is urgently needed. The democratically elected Global Government in the World of a little less than 7 billion (700 crore) people would have one representative at every ten million (one crore) people.

It would be imperative for the new leadership to solve the problem of unemployment taking it as a prime objective of the planning not as a by-product of the process of the development. In the World of today, to save the people and the system from the greed of individuals and the corporate world, the Global Democratic Government would be formed sooner or latter. There are so many problems in the World which need urgent attention and none is to take care of. Policy of the protectionism can not be a solution. The hard work, honesty, self-restrain, fairness and integrity under the competent global leadership can bring back the trust, the confidence and the momentum in the global economy and in the World.

the mass of production during the last a few centuries. It has provided bed-rock and strength to the global economy.

The 19th century industrial capitalism was organized around the standardized mass production, scale economies and the mass consumption. In 20th century, with the changes in the technology, the orientation of the industrial capitalism changed into the 'flexible' production, innovation, scope economies and the differentiated pattern of the consumption.

The information and communication revolution with the global networking of computers has drastically changed the global scenario. After the computer revolution, digitalization, electronic information processing technologies and tendencies, the financial and industrial capitalism revolutionized the different processes of the global economy. Significant changes have occurred in the processes of the production, distribution, exchange and so on.

The capitalism, whether it is financial or industrial, in the 21st century, has become disorganized with the decreasing national regulations. The global capitalists and the multinational companies have monopolized the production of the goods and services. The monopoly of the multinational corporations in the field of the real economy has resulted into the decrease in number of the small and the medium entrepreneurs who have to play very important role in the global economy.

The monopoly of the multinational corporations has controlled in the economy but could not generate the required quantum of the employment. The economic growth took place, the production and the productivity increased but at the same time unemployment also increased. Consequently, the benefits of the growth went in a few hands and caused the concentration of the wealth.

By close of the 20th century, a situation arose in which the huge production with high productivity was achieved in the economy but the masses suffered from the unemployment and under employment. Therefore, they did not have money to

References

Ahssan, M.H, Recession in India: Challenges and Opportunities Galore, December 22, 2008.

Business Week: A New World Economy-The Balance of Power will Shift to the East as China and India Evolve, August 22, 2005.

Clark, Andrew, U.S. Firms Queue up for Bailouts, The Hindu, Thursday, December 25, 2008.

Cooke, Terry, E-Notes: Asia's Economy: Challenge and Opportunity for Obama Administration, February 2009.

Data and Research, Historic Commodity Price Boom ends with Slowing Global Growth, December 9, 2008, Global Economic Prospects, 2009, World Bank.

Dejardin, Amelita King, Economic Meltdown-This Crisis has a Woman's Face, The Hindu, Saturday, March 7, 2009.

Dikshit, Ramesh Dutta, Political Geography-The Discipline and its Dimensions, 2nd ed. 1994, Tata McGraw-Hill Publishing Company Limited, New Delhi.

Economic Survey of India, (*various issues*).

Elliott, Larry, Davos: How to Regain People's Trust?, The Hindu, Tuesday, February 3, 2009.

Hartshorn, Truman A. and Alexander, John W., Economic Geography, 3rd ed., December 1992, Prentice-Hall of India Pvt. Ltd.

Katju, Markandey, Reflections on the Global Economic Crisis, The Hindu, Monday, March 9, 2009.

Konana, Prabhu Dev, Anarchic Capitalism vs. Sensible Capitalism, The Hindu, Thursday, December 4, 2008.

Konicz, Tomasz, From Real Estate Speculation to Collapse of Global Deficit Economy-Short History of the Worldwide Economic Crisis, Part 3, Friday, January 2, 2009.

Kromm, David E., World Regional Geography, Kansas State University, Kansas, the U.S. Saunders College, 1981.

Kulkarni, M.R., Industrial Development, National Book Trust, India, 1991.

Maddison, Angus, The World Economy-A Millennial Perspective, Paris, OECD 2001.

Nehru, Pt. Jawahar Lal, Glimpses of World History, Penguin Books India, 2004.

Patnaik, Utsa, Behind the Triple Global Crisis, The Hindu Tuesday, November 4, 2008.

Paul, James and Heikki, Patomaki, Capitalism: Beyond All or Nothing Arguments, Globalization and Finance.

Rangarajan, C., Capitalism and Economic Crisis, The Hindu, May 11, 2009.

Rangarajan, C., The Financial Crisis and its Ramifications, The Hindu, November 08, 2008.

Sainath, P., U.S. Economy-It's Business as Unusual, The Hindu, December 27, 2008.

Shah, Anup, Global Financial Crisis 2008-Global Issues, December 07, 2008.

Shah, Anup, Poverty Facts and States-Global Issues, September 03, 2008.

Silva, Luiz Inacio, Lula da, The BRIC Comes of Age, The Hindu, June 16, 2009.

Stiglitz, Joseph- What I learned at the World Economic Crisis- The Insider, The New Republic April 17 2000.

The Collapse of Manufacturing-February 19, 2009, Economist.

The Impact of Financial Crisis on Low Income Countries Brookings Institution, March 19, 2009.

Venkitaraman, S., Saturday, Global Financial Crisis: Reflections on its Impact on India, The Hindu, October 18, 2008.

Vidal, Jon, Thursday, Year of Interlinked Food Shortage, Climate Change and Recession, The Hindu, December 18, 2008.

Wikipedia, the free encyclopaedia, Sub-prime mortgage Crisis, Economic History of the United States, World Government, Derivative (Finance), Panic of 1871, Great

Depression, Bretton Woods System, 1994 Economic Crisis in Mexico, 1997Asian Finance Crisis, Bio-fuel in the United States, Food Security, World Population and Poverty, List of countries by GDP (PPP), Afghanistan.

frequently used in the present day derivative markets. The contracts to buy and sell an asset on or before a future date at a price specified today are called futures and forwards. Options give owners the right but not the obligations to buy and or sell an asset. When parties enter into an option price is specified. Swaps are the contracts to exchange cash on or before a specified future date.

The contracts which are negotiated privately and traded directly between the two parties without going through exchange or any other intermediary are called the over-the-counter (OTC) contracts. The OTC contract market is largely made up of sophisticated parties like the banks and the hedge funds. The OTCs are largely un-regulated disclosures of information between the parties.

The derivatives mainly leverage the debt in an economy. They create even more difficulty for underlying real economy to service its debt obligations and to curtail the real economic activities which can cause a recession in the economy.

The credit default swap is an insurance contract between a protection buyer and a protection seller covering a corporation's (the referenced entity) specific bond or loan. It is an OTC contract and could be sold to another party. The protection buyer pays an upfront amount and an annual premium to the protection seller to cover any loss on the face amount of the referenced bond or loan.

The credit default swaps are not standardized instruments, not securities technically, not transparent, not traded on exchange, not subject to the present securities law, not regulated and so on.

Paul B. Farrel wrote in an article titled- "Derivatives the new ticking bomb", on March 10, 2008.

"The fact is derivatives have become world's newest and biggest black market exceeding the illicit traffic in stuff like arms, drugs, alcohols, gambling, cigarettes, stolen art and pirated movies. Why? Because like all black market, derivatives are perfect way of getting rich while avoiding taxes

Index

corporate governance and the increased accountability of the officers and the boards of the directors of the publicly traded companies. The importance of the audit committee must improve and penalties for the corporate misconduct must intensify.